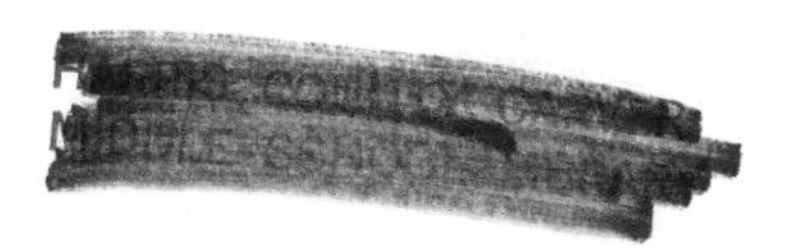

You Are the General

You Are the General

Nathan Aaseng

The Oliver Press, Inc.
Minneapolis

The Oliver Press
Josiah King House
2709 Lyndale Avenue South
Minneapolis, MN 55408

Library of Congress Cataloging-in-Publication Data

Aaseng, Nathan
You are the general / Nathan Aaseng.

p. cm. — (Great decisions)
Includes bibliographical references and index.
Summary: Examines great military decisions of the twentieth century.
ISBN 1-881508-11-0 : $14.95
1. Military policy—Decision making—Juvenile literature.
[1. Military policy.] I. Title. II. Series.
UA11. A27 1994 93-11661
355'.0335—dc20 CIP
AC

ISBN: 1-881508-11-0
Great Decisions II
Printed in the United States of America

99 98 97 96 95 94 8 7 6 5 4 3 2 1

Contents

A graduate and later the superintendent of the United States Military Academy at West Point, New York, Douglas MacArthur spent nearly a half century in the army, serving his country with distinction in three wars.

INTRODUCTION

This is the moment you have trained for all of your life, but you hoped it would never arrive. War has broken out. Your country is engaged in a life-and-death struggle—and you are in command!

In the midst of this conflict, you run into a prickly situation that calls for decisive action. As you ponder your options for dealing with this matter, you realize you are standing at the crossroads of history. The choice you make may decide the outcome of the conflict. The lives of your soldiers—and perhaps even the fate of millions of people—depend on your decision.

No one else can make the decision. You can listen to advice and consult maps and intelligence reports, but in the end you will have to give the orders. And you dare not be wrong!

As a military commander, you need to be something of a gambler, for war holds no certainties. You know that the best-laid plans of military geniuses can blow up in their faces. As United States Admiral Raymond Spruance wrote after fighting in one of the key battles of World

War II, "I am more than ever impressed with the part that good or bad fortune sometimes plays in tactical engagements." Luck is something you cannot control. Nevertheless, if your choice turns out badly, for whatever reason, the blame lies with you because the decision was yours.

This book presents a wide spectrum of military quandaries of the twentieth century. Some chapters will ask you to plot master strategies that involve moving armies across an entire continent. Others will ask for decisions on where to deploy your troops on smaller battlefields or on the sea. You will decide when and where to attack. You must determine when to take extra precautions and when to take risks.

Throughout the seven chapters of this book, you command a variety of military forces from several different nations. You will put yourself in the place of those you may admire and those you may despise. By getting inside their minds, you will see how the history of the world has taken shape and how history could have been different. You will discover what might have happened if you had been in command.

1

The Kaiser's Army

August 1914

War has been brewing for years in central Europe. In preparation for the moment when the minor disputes and incidents might explode into war, nations have been amassing armies, stockpiling weapons, drawing up military plans, and forging alliances for several decades.

One source of conflict is a long-standing feud between Germany and France. The two dominant powers of the continent have quarreled over such things as the location of their common boundary. Their disputes flared into a war in 1870. When Germany won that conflict, Europe split into two camps. The humiliated French and the suspicious Russians formed an alliance to protect themselves from the power of Germany and its partner, Austria-Hungary, while Italy leaned toward the side of

Germany. Meanwhile, Great Britain began to edge closer to its historical enemy—France.

On June 28, 1914, a revolutionary from the small country of Serbia assassinated Austria-Hungary's Archduke Franz Ferdinand. When Austria-Hungary

Kaiser Wilhelm I (1797-1888) led Germany to victory over France in their war of 1870-71, sowing seeds of bitterness between the two countries that contributed to the outbreak of the First World War.

declared war on Serbia, Russia came to the aid of the smaller Serbia. That brought the two main European alliances into conflict. Germany entered the war on the side of Austria-Hungary; France came in on the side of Russia. Presently, both Great Britain and Italy are staying neutral.

Russia is a vast country, and its leaders will require some time to gather their troops and organize an attack against Germany. In addition, because Russia will have to contend with the armies of Austria-Hungary, you don't need to worry much about Germany's eastern border. The most immediate concern for your German armies is the French. Their powerful forces are in place and ready to fight along your western border.

One of the most basic military decisions involves whether to fight an offensive war (attack) or a defensive war (defend against an enemy attack). The French-German border is a relatively short stretch of land bounded on the north by the countries of Luxembourg and Belgium, and on the south by the mountains of Switzerland. A short border gives the advantage to the defenders even against a superior army. Such a border allows the defenders to concentrate their forces in well-protected positions and leaves little room for the attackers to maneuver.

Your border with France—the western front—is now brimming with armies and weapons more powerful than anything the world has ever seen. The actions taken on that front in the next few months will decide the fate of Europe.

THE OPPOSING FORCES

With a population of 37 million people, France has about two-thirds the manpower available to Germany. Smarter from their defeat in 1870, the French have worked hard at building up their armed forces. Their army has swelled to more than 1 million soldiers. Most of the soldiers are stationed near the German border, where their positions are protected by a series of well-prepared forts.

The 1870 defeat left psychological scars on the French. In an effort to explain their defeat, they blamed the defensive strategy used by their generals. Ever since then, they have emphasized the need to seize the offensive against Germany. According to their leaders, the "French temperament" is better suited to glorious mass charges than to defensive tactics. As a symbol of their fearless, aggressive attitude, the French continue to wear their traditional brightly colored uniforms that include red pants.

Since the glory days of Napoleon 100 years ago, French generals have been mediocre at best. The effects of poor leadership continue to show. According to a report prepared for your armies, the French army is "not sufficiently trained for a major war."

This same report praises the skill, enthusiasm, and intelligence of the French soldiers whose patriotism often spurs them to heroic deeds. But it criticizes their training, discipline, and ability to weather tough situations.

YOUR FORCES

You can put at least 2 million soldiers into action and get them into position quickly. Most military experts agree that Germany has the best-trained, best-equipped, and most efficient fighting force in the world. Both the German generals and their soldiers have performed brilliantly in recent campaigns. They have acted boldly, winning quick, decisive victories with a minimum of losses. Their success has given them enormous confidence in their superiority over the French army.

You have adapted somewhat more readily to modern warfare than have the French. Your gray uniforms blend in well with the surroundings, so you do not present an obvious target to the enemy. Steel helmets give you better protection than the soft headgear worn by the French. You have also trained your troops to use the protection of the land rather than charge into the open.

Because of political concerns, the one area of military expertise in which you may be at a disadvantage is in your chain of command: The German crown prince commands one of your eight armies, and the duke of Wurtemburg commands another. Royalty are not accustomed to taking orders. If you offend them, they can take their complaints straight to Kaiser Wilhelm II, the emperor of Germany.

YOU ARE IN COMMAND.

What strategy will you use to defeat the French?

Option 1 **Carry out the Schlieffen Plan.**

There are basically two ways to defeat a strong army: break through the line at some point, or maneuver around one of its ends ("flanks") so you can attack and surround the army from behind.

Graf Alfred von Schlieffen, who retired from the German general staff in 1906, formulated a flanking maneuver known as the Schlieffen Plan. Von Schlieffen argued that the short frontier along the French-German border would be too difficult to break through without heavy losses. The best way to defeat the French was to use a flanking maneuver—attack from the north through Belgium, a flat country with a network of good roads that would allow troops to move quickly.

The key to the Schlieffen Plan is a massive attack by the German right wing. In fact, von Schlieffen was so insistent on this point that on his death bed he uttered the words, "Keep the right wing strong." He proposed to keep a small defensive force along the French-German border. The French could attack and even push the German defenders back a short distance. That was not a concern because, while that small force remained stationary, the right wing of the German army would swing around through Belgium and slam into the rear of the French. This plan would widen the front, give the superior German army room to maneuver, and stretch the weaker French forces across terrain that would be difficult to defend.

There is, however, a danger in leaving your thin defensive line along the border at risk for too long. If the right wing's drive stalls, the French may have time to break through into Germany and disrupt your plans. But if you put an overwhelming majority of your forces on that right wing, you should not have to worry about stalling. Your armies will be able to simply push straight ahead and collapse the French left wing. The French armies defending their border would then have to retreat or be caught and crushed in a vise, as the right wing of the German army closes in behind them.

Of course, the Belgians would not appreciate being used as a highway. But that tiny country has only a small army of 165,000, which the German forces could easily sweep aside.

***Option 2* Order a modified, flexible Schlieffen Plan.**

The Schlieffen Plan contains risks that might call for a slight adjustment. First, it trusts the defense of your borders to a small portion of your armies. The short French-German border may favor you as the defender, but it does not make you invincible. With the French being so determined to take the offensive in this war, your border troops are sure to come under heavy attack. Von Schlieffen had been willing to allow the French to capture some German territory, believing they could not penetrate far before your right wing overwhelmed them. But he retired eight years ago, and the French are stronger now than they were when he made his plan.

As chief of the German general staff, Field Marshal Alfred von Schlieffen (1833-1913) designed a strategy to defeat France in the event of a future war between the long-time European rivals.

Also, the Schlieffen Plan calls for so many troops on your right wing that only a small force would be left on your eastern borders to deal with whatever early threat the Russians might mount. Von Schlieffen was willing to abandon German territory in East Prussia to the Russians because he believed the important task was to defeat France. He calculated that even a small German army could delay the Russians until that was accomplished. Then Germany could turn on Russia and defeat its armies easily.

The military prestige of Russia has been tarnished by its recent loss to Japan in the Russo-Japanese War. But does the Schlieffen Plan dangerously underestimate a country as huge as Russia? Is leaving Germany exposed to a Russian attack wise? Don't the German people deserve some insurance against invasion?

Another objection to the original Schlieffen Plan comes from an offensive point of view. Although you could gain a victory by overturning the French flank with your right wing, that might not give you a complete victory. Much of the French army could retreat to the south and set up a new line of defense. But if you achieved a small breakthrough on your left wing at the same time, you could bottle up the French completely. They would have no choice but to surrender.

The French might be so frantic to stop your right wing's advance that they would pull troops away from the French-German border to deal with them. That could give you the opening you need. Although it would slightly weaken your right wing, it might be worth taking some troops from that wing and placing them on the left for this breakthrough.

Option 3 Attack the defenses at the French-German border.

The main problem with either version of the Schlieffen Plan is the march through Belgium, a neutral country. A 1839 treaty signed by Great Britain and other nations had guaranteed respect for Belgium's borders. By violating that treaty, you risk bringing Great Britain into the war against you.

Although it favors France in its dispute with Germany, Great Britain has so far stayed out of the conflict. Furthermore, Great Britain and Germany have a long history of good relations. On the other hand, Great Britain and France have been enemies for centuries. A good chance exists that the British will sit out this war as long as you do not provoke them by running roughshod over Belgium. Great Britain's small army does not scare you, but its powerful navy could cause difficulty for you if the war continues to escalate.

Another problem with the Schlieffen Plan is that it is no secret. The French have known about it for years, ever since a disgruntled German officer divulged it to them. If the French know what to expect, they surely have prepared an adequate defense against it.

While an attack on the French defensive lines at the French-German border may be costly, that may be exactly what the French do not expect. At any rate, you can trust the superiority of your forces to carry the day.

Option 4 **Wait for a French attack; then crush it and and counterattack.**

This option allows you to take advantage of a French weakness. By playing on the French obsession with fighting an offensive war, this plan could avoid two negatives: the massive loss of life of a German frontal assault on the French-German border and the march through Belgium that could bring Great Britain into the fighting against you.

The French leaders have not adapted their tactics to the realities of modern war. Their soldiers still march out in the open in their bright uniforms, making them clear targets. Their generals still believe in mass charges of infantry and cavalry against strong defensive positions, believing they can triumph through the sheer force of willpower and patriotism.

The French do not realize that these tactics have been obsolete for at least 60 years. The mass charge may have worked fine in the days of swords and single-shot rifles. But because a modern army can fire so much ammunition so quickly, frontal assaults have become sheer suicide.

Since the French plan to attack anyway, the best plan would be to lay a trap for them. Let them dash out from their fortifications in one of their glorious charges. Then, if you retreat from the first wave of assaults, perhaps the French will become overconfident and pour more troops into an increasingly reckless offensive.

Meanwhile, you can have a second, stronger line of defense waiting for the French. When they reach this line, you can use your modern firepower to cut them to

Kaiser Wilhelm II (1859-1941), grandson of Wilhelm I, sat on the German throne from 1888 to 1918.

shreds. At that point, the French can either lose their army on the field or retreat headlong back home across the border. Your army can counterattack, hot on their heels. The enemy's confusion, decimated ranks, and shattered spirit should make their defenses far easier to breach than if you had simply attacked them at the start.

THE DECISION IS YOURS.
WHAT WILL YOU DO?

Option 1 **Carry out the Schlieffen Plan.**

Option 2 **Order a modified, flexible Schlieffen Plan.**

Option 3 **Attack the defenses at the French-German border.**

Option 4 **Wait for a French attack; then crush it and counterattack.**

Helmuth von Moltke (1848-1916) was a veteran of Germany's 1870 war with France. He followed von Schlieffen as chief of the general staff and took over the responsibility for carrying out his predecessor's war plans.

The German commander, Helmuth von Moltke, chose *Option 2*.

Von Moltke began by following the Schlieffen Plan. He divided his forces into eight armies and assigned five of these armies (totalling more than 1.1 million men) to the marching right wing. Next, he gave two armies the task of defending the French-German border. A single army patrolled the eastern front against the Russians.

Before the start of the battle, von Moltke had second thoughts about the weak border defenses against France, so he shifted some troops from the marching right wing to the left. After launching his attack, von Moltke worried about reports that Russian soldiers had advanced into East Prussia and pushed back the German defenders. He further weakened his five right-wing armies by shifting some of their sections to the eastern front.

As his right wing advanced on the French forces, von Moltke ordered his center and left wing to attack weak points in the French lines. If successful, this attack would envelop the entire French army and capture a million prisoners in the greatest military victory of all time.

RESULT

German troops stormed through Belgium in early August, brushing past the heroic but futile resistance of the small Belgian army. As anticipated, this move brought Great Britain into the war against Germany. The British quickly dispatched a small force of 80,000 soldiers to join the French army.

In a series of bitter clashes in late August, the defensive forces holding down Germany's left wing shattered France's obsolete mass offensive. Meanwhile, the powerful German right wing swept down into France. It soundly defeated the French armies in the left and center and forced them to retreat. German troops pursued the fleeing enemy relentlessly through northern France to the outskirts of Paris. As they reached the capital, the French troops were exhausted and demoralized.

By the end of August, the German plan had nearly achieved total victory. The French army was being squeezed in a vice, and Paris was ready to fall. Furthermore, the British troops were so demoralized that their leader wanted to pull them out of the battle.

The German right wing, however, did not have quite enough troops to engulf Paris without opening dangerous gaps in their lines. This shortage of soldiers forced them to close their ranks and bypass Paris as they tried to surround the French armies.

Meanwhile, the French siphoned off some forces from their right to create a new army to the west near Paris. This army attacked the onrushing German right wing by surprise from the side. The rest of the retreating

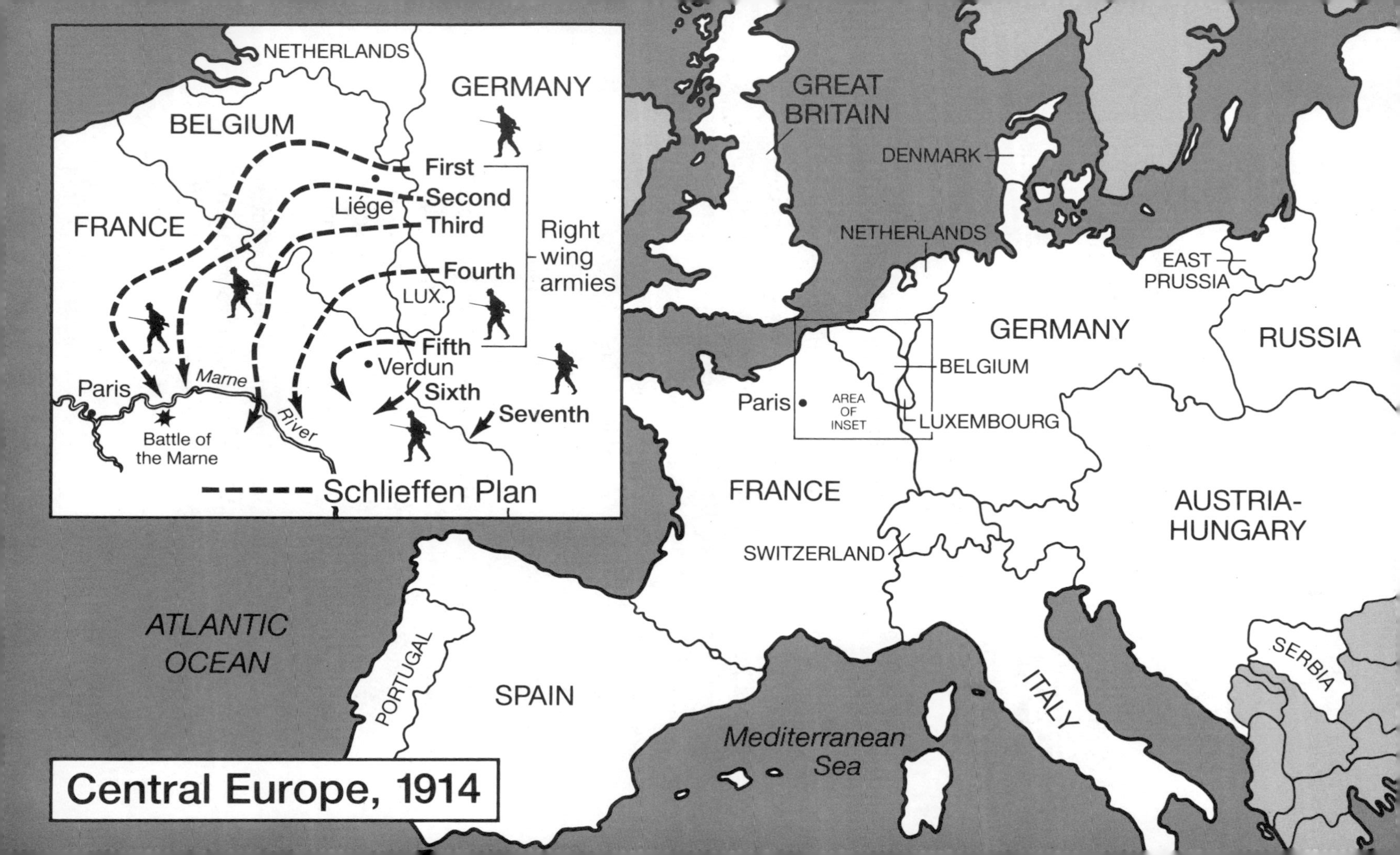

Central Europe, 1914

French army then turned and attacked German forces all along the front in what came to be called the Battle of the Marne, named after a river close to the battlefront.

Suddenly, the Germans were the ones in danger of being taken from the rear. So near to victory, the Germans were forced to retreat to escape the trap they had fallen into. Only a valiant effort by a small German corps and a too-slow advance by the British army saved the German army from utter catastrophe.

ANALYSIS

The Schlieffen Plan was a bold offensive designed to defeat France quickly. Von Moltke made a fatal error by backing down from von Schlieffen's insistence that the right wing had to be strengthened at all costs. Von Moltke failed to heed Napoleon's advice that "when you give battle, muster all your forces, omitting none; a single battalion sometimes wins the day."

Von Moltke stripped his right wing of the forces that might have allowed it to complete its job. Worse yet, his weakening of the right wing was unnecessary. The small German army on the eastern front defeated the Russian army and stopped its advance before the reinforcements from the right wing arrived. Similarly, the German defensive left wing did not need extra soldiers to hold the border against the French, who never came close to breaking through.

The Germans clearly had the French on the run at the end of August. With a few more troops, their right wing could have captured Paris and kept surrounding the

French army. Had they finished the job, Germany could have dictated its own terms to the beaten French and dominated the continent for decades to come. Instead, the German armies lost the Battle of the Marne and got bogged down in a bloody trench war in which neither side could gain ground.

Von Schlieffen proved to be correct in dismissing the Russian threat as minor. Within three years, the Russian army collapsed and the Bolshevik Revolution tore apart the country and ended its involvement in the war.

In the early weeks of the war, Germany might have been able to take advantage of France's ill-advised and outdated offensive tactics by luring its armies into a trap, destroying them, and then counterattacking. The disastrous French offensive in August proved how foolish their initial ideas had been. But they learned from their mistakes and the same opportunity would not be available to the Germans again.

Having failed to win a quick victory, the Germans paid the price of their attack through Belgium. Great Britain's rebuilt army and powerful navy helped equalize the Germans' military edge over the French. The war dragged on for three more years until the United States joined in on the side of France and Great Britain. By then, Germany's defeat was inevitable.

The disaster at the Marne destroyed von Moltke, and he was relieved of his command following the battle. Shattered by his failure, he fell ill and died before the end of the war.

Perhaps the most disastrous outcome of his mistake was its effect on the German people. Their armies had been surging toward an overwhelming victory against France. Then suddenly their armies retreated. Bewildered by the change of fortune so incredible that the French called it the "Miracle of the Marne," many Germans believed that their leaders had betrayed their army. Still convinced that their armies were invincible, they never accepted the surrender imposed on them by France and its allies at the end of the war.

Within a short time, a man named Adolf Hitler would use German resentment at being "stabbed in the back" to wreak revenge on the French in World War II.

2

THE ARMIES OF THE GERMAN REICH

Summer 1940

Your armies have overrun your European neighbors, blowing through their defenses as though they were made of straw. A year ago, your lightning war (blitzkrieg) conquered Poland. Earlier this spring, your armies seized Denmark and most of Norway. Then, on May 10, 1940, you unleashed another lightning attack on the nations to your west. The Netherlands fell within a week; Belgium, within three weeks.

Most military experts expected Great Britain and France to join together to make a strong stand against you. Yet at the end of May, you trapped a large British army at Dunkirk on the coast of France. The British escaped by the skin of their teeth, ferried home on a hastily assembled collection of whatever floating craft could be found in England. You followed that success by shattering the French army, supposedly the most powerful land force in the world. On June 14, the French surrendered their capital of Paris without a fight. A week later, the French government surrendered.

France fell so suddenly and so unexpectedly that you are undecided as to what Germany should do next. For even though Germany is now the undisputed master of central and western Europe, you cannot afford to be overconfident. Your aggressive military actions have made many enemies who could cause trouble for you in the future.

THE OPPOSING FORCES

To the northwest lies Great Britain. While severely battered, this small island nation is the only country officially at war with you. Its ground forces are no match for yours, as you proved in action around Dunkirk. Your troops are far more numerous and better equipped, especially since you forced the British to abandon virtually all their modern tanks and heavy artillery at Dunkirk. At the moment, the shorthanded British army is reeling in confusion after its disastrous defeat.

Yet, Great Britain remains a foe that bears watching. It still commands a powerful navy and has built up a respectable air force. Traditionally, the country is a strong military power that could pose an immediate threat because its land lies just a few miles off the coast of your newly acquired territory in France.

From May 26 to June 4, 1940, more than 200,000 British and 100,000 French and Belgian soldiers were rescued from the Dunkirk beaches in northern France.

The British also maintain a strong military presence to the south of your territory. Their ships patrol the Mediterranean Sea, and their garrisons control key posts that guard it: Gibraltar and Suez at either end of the sea, the islands of Crete and Malta, as well as sections of North Africa in between. British forces in these areas could possibly mount a threat to your southern borders.

Your eastern borders lie under the shadow of Soviet Russia, ruled by the Communist dictator Josef Stalin. Your country is not at war with the Russians—in fact, you recently signed a nonaggression pact with them that divided Poland between the two of you. But your country despises this giant nation and the Communist philosophy that it preaches.

Recently, Russia has been bullying its neighbors and prowling near your territories. Its army is enormous—larger than yours, though not as well trained or well equipped. Russia's air force is only adequate, and naval forces would not be a factor in a war over the broad plains and forests of western Russia.

In a recent border war with Finland, Russia fought poorly. Although the Russian forces eventually captured a small piece of Finnish territory, they suffered casualties three times those of the badly outnumbered Finns.

Standing on the sidelines is the foe you most fear: the United States. Should the United States ever decide to enter the war against you, the country's tremendous industrial capacity to produce war materials could have a devastating effect. The Americans are on friendly terms with Great Britain, while they distrust both Germany and Russia. But at present, the United States is reluctant to get involved in any foreign wars.

YOUR FORCES

No nation can match the strength, training, and discipline of the German ground forces. You can put more than 2 million soldiers in the field at any location in Europe. Your armored tank divisions are first-rate. Your air force, too, looks invincible, but it has not really been tested. Its stunning success early in this war came against weak opposition. Your navy cannot begin to match the British fleet.

You could easily overwhelm the British forces in the Mediterranean, and you are probably strong enough to defeat the Russian army. Your forces could also destroy the army defending Britain, if you can get your troops across the English Channel onto British soil. But you would be asking too much if you demanded a decisive victory in more than one place at a time.

Germany has made military alliances with Japan and Italy, but Japan is too far away to affect your immediate concerns. Italy lies to the south of you, along the Mediterranean Sea, and could take on a major share of the fighting in that area. You have serious concerns, however, about the effectiveness of the Italian armed forces.

The Russians have angered and intimidated a number of their smaller neighbors, such as Finland and Rumania. You could expect these countries to contribute to your attack on Russia, but neither are major military powers.

Soviet Russia's leader, Josef Stalin (right), and Germany's foreign minister, Joachim von Ribbentrop, in Moscow after signing the August 1939 non-aggression pact between their countries

YOU ARE IN COMMAND.

Decisive victories mean nothing unless you can use them to your advantage. Where will you concentrate your major effort in the next phase of the war?

Option 1 **Invade Great Britain.**

The British are your only declared enemies at the moment. They are all that stands between you and total control of Europe. Now, while they are battered, poorly equipped, and disorganized, is the time to eliminate them as a threat. All you need to do is land enough troops in Great Britain, either by parachute or by boat, to capture a small beachhead. The British are so short of tanks, artillery, and trained reserve units that they will never be able to stop your superior ground forces once they are established.

The British, however, are tough and resilient. If you let them off the hook now, they could recover their strength and pose a serious threat to you, especially if they coax the United States into joining their war effort. Eliminating Great Britain will remove the threat of invasion from the West because even the United States could not launch a European invasion from across the Atlantic Ocean. That action would free you to accomplish whatever you want in the East and in the Mediterranean.

This option, however, has a negative side. Those few miles of water between England and your forces in France pose a greater risk than anything you have faced so far in the war. Crossing the English Channel is dangerous when the enemy boasts the stronger navy. Most of your naval commanders are leery of the task.

Your air force could neutralize Great Britain's sea advantage. Air strikes could target and destroy British ships and war industry factories, while air transport planes could land paratroopers. That strategy, however, depends on the ability of your pilots to wrest control of the sky from the British Royal Air Force for at least a brief period.

Another strong reason for avoiding an invasion is that the British are in such desperate straits that you may be able to force their surrender without risking your armies. Perhaps you could negotiate a peace. Surely the British know their position is hopeless. Hardly anyone outside Great Britain believes the British can hold out for more than a few weeks. Rather than allow themselves to be destroyed, the British might accept conditions of surrender, especially if those terms are favorable. Your government is quite willing to be generous. The Germans have far more respect for the British than for any of the other peoples that surround them. They would welcome an alliance and allow them to retain their government.

If the British choose to be stubborn, you could apply pressure in other ways. Great Britain is a small island that depends on supplies from overseas. You could attack British ships and prevent them from bringing in any supplies. Furthermore, Great Britain is within easy range of your bombers. You could pulverize factories, ports—even whole cities—until the British finally beg for peace. This strategy, however, goes against a 1938 German military study that warned that air attacks were likely to make the

British even more determined to fight and that ground forces would be needed to force the British to surrender.

So far, Great Britain has only resisted the peace offers and threats from Germany. Britain's new prime minister, Winston Churchill, has stated, "Let it end only when each one of us lies choking in his own blood upon the ground."

Option 2 **Invade Russia.**

You may not be at war with Russia, but that does not mean you can trust its premier, Josef Stalin. Stalin is a cold, ruthless killer who has executed thousands of his enemies in Russia. In the past months, he has nibbled at territory near your eastern borders. In October of last year, he bullied the tiny Baltic states of Estonia, Latvia, and Lithuania into allowing the Soviet Union to station troops on their territory, and now he is trying to annex them entirely. His forces also attacked Finland and occupied a portion of Rumania. If you concentrate your forces on invading Great Britain, Stalin might take advantage of your weakness on the eastern front and attack you.

Germany and the United States share a common dislike of the Communist government of Russia. Both countries believe the Communists have been causing disturbances in the hope of creating a world revolution. Germany could gain favor with the Americans by destroying the Communist menace. At the very least, the United States would be less likely to support the Russians than they would the British.

Realistically, the huge armies of Russia pose the only present threat to your security. Once you destroy them, your control over the European mainland will be complete. As an added bonus, the Soviet Union is rich in resources. The vast agricultural region of the Ukraine could take care of all your food needs, while other areas of Russia could provide oil and minerals to keep your military machine going.

In addition, an attack on Russia does not require passage over a channel of water. All that lies between your armies and Moscow, the capital of Soviet Russia, are open plains, forests, rivers, and a large army. Based on the success of your troops against France and Poland and the failure of the Russian troops against Finland, your soldiers should cut through Russia with ease.

On the negative side, if your troops do not smash through to a quick victory, this strategy could be a terrible mistake. If the British get back on their feet at home and hold onto their territory in the Mediterranean while the Russians hold off your advance, you will be forced to fight on at least two fronts—possibly three. Your armies would be stretched thin as they simultaneously try to defend your positions in the east, west, and south.

The Russians have some factors in their favor. Their poor showing against Finland alerted them to their military weaknesses, and they have been working hard to shore up their troops. The vast plains of Russia would provide an enormous theater of war that could stretch the battlefront for more than 2,000 miles. This would give an advantage to the side with the most soldiers—Russia. Roads in this vast country are few and poorly maintained, which negates the advantage of the more highly mechanized and mobile German units. Weather is

Central Europe, 1940

also on the Russians' side. If they can stall your advance long enough, your troops would be stuck on the freezing plains in front of Moscow with no protection from the brutal cold.

Option 3 **Secure the Mediterranean Sea.**

This would likely be the easiest of the three campaigns to win. You could keep enough troops along the eastern border to discourage Russian advances while still massing enough force to clean the British out of their numerous pockets in the Mediterranean. The British cannot begin to match the number of infantry and tank divisions that you could send to this area.

Your advisers are constantly warning you of the strategic importance of the Mediterranean. German control of islands and ports would deny the British fleet any bases from which to operate and would turn the whole Mediterranean into a "German lake." This would protect your southern borders, which would be vulnerable to attack should your Italian allies falter.

Among the disadvantages of this strategy is the fact that such an effort would step on the toes of some friends. You would have to march through Spain to seize Gibraltar. Spain's government has been friendly to you in the past, but it does not want your armies inside its borders. Your Italian allies have dreams of creating their own empire around the Mediterranean and have urged you to give them free reign in North Africa. This does not bother you because, like most Germans, you believe "the Mediterranean countries have always been death to the Germans." You would be happy to let the Italians do the fighting down there as long as they can back up their claims of military might.

Another problem with this option is that it leaves your most dangerous enemies—Great Britain and Russia—undisturbed.

Option 4 **Hold your ground and consolidate your winnings.**

Germany went to war before its military was fully prepared. So far, it has been fortunate enough to benefit from the weaknesses and errors of Germany's enemies in the past few years. But the German army's reorganization is not scheduled to be completed until 1943, and target dates for bringing the air force and navy up to standards are even farther away.

Some advisers believe you should use this time to regroup and build up your war industries and armed forces. Others argue that you dare not idle away the great advantage you have gained by your victories.

THE DECISION IS YOURS. WHAT WILL YOU DO?

Option 1 **Invade Great Britain.**

Option 2 **Invade Russia.**

Option 3 **Secure the Mediterranean Sea.**

Option 4 **Hold your ground and consolidate your winnings.**

Although he served only as an enlisted man in World War I, Adolf Hitler ultimately commanded all of the German military forces in World War II.

Adolf Hitler, the supreme commander of the German forces, chose *Option 2.*

Hitler believed that Great Britain was too badly defeated to pose a further threat to him. "The British have lost the war, but they don't know it. One must give them time, and they will come around," he declared after Dunkirk.

Because of Hitler's respect for Great Britain, he wished to avoid conquering it, an act that he believed would be "detrimental to the white race." Instead, he told aides that he would "come to an understanding with Great Britain." One of the few times he dawdled during the war was while trying to entice the British with peace offers.

Even when that failed, Hitler held off on an invasion. According to an adviser, "crossing the channel appears very hazardous to [Hitler]. On that account, invasion is to be undertaken only if no other means is left to come to terms with Great Britain." Instead of invading, Hitler tried to force Britain's surrender by cutting off its supplies and bombing its factories. The Germans did develop an invasion plan, but they never made it a top priority and never attempted it.

Hitler made similar advances in the Mediterranean, but he never gave priority to that region. German armies did not threaten Gibraltar or the Suez, and their North African troops were sparse and poorly supplied.

Hitler, who was too aggressive in nature to pull back or stand still in the middle of a war, chose to attack Russia. In the summer of 1940, he ordered German generals to prepare plans for an invasion to take place in the spring of 1941. Hitler was convinced that he could overwhelm the Russians in a quick, furious campaign. Once that was completed, he could concentrate on Great Britain, which would then be totally isolated.

On June 22, 1941, the German army stormed into Russia.

Hitler and Hermann Göring, leader of the Luftwaffe (German air force), greet a parade of Nazi followers.

RESULT

With devastating force, the German army hurled back the Russian army all along a 2,000-mile front. In ten weeks, the Germans drove hundreds of miles into Russian territory, causing more than a million Russian casualties. Although reeling badly, the retreating Russian army kept throwing fresh reserves at the Germans. The Russians suffered terrible losses, but Germany also began to lose many soldiers.

That autumn, Hitler made the mistake of halting the German army's advance long enough to encircle a large Russian army. Although the two-week operation captured or killed roughly a million Russians, it put the invasion behind schedule. By the time the Germans drew near Moscow in early December, the weather had turned against them. Muddy roads followed by sub-zero temperatures caught the invaders unprepared. Ill-clad German soldiers froze on the front lines, and their tanks and trucks stalled in the cold.

The failure to capture Moscow before winter proved disastrous. The Russians had time to regroup and counterattack. Hitler compounded his error with further mistakes later in the campaign. Eventually, a disastrous defeat at Stalingrad in January 1943 forced the Germans to retreat.

Meanwhile the United States, which had declared war on Germany on December 11, 1941, had joined Britain in driving the outgunned Germans and Italians from North Africa in 1942. Working from the south, the Allied forces crossed the Mediterranean, invading

Italy and forcing the Italians out of the war. In 1944, the British and Americans used Great Britain—still unconquered—as a base for an invasion of the western European mainland.

By June of 1944, Germany had put itself in the almost impossible position of trying to fight a war on three fronts—Russian, Italian, and French—at the same time. From that point on, defeat was inevitable.

Their army destroyed, dozens of the 90,000 German prisoners trudge through the snows of Stalingrad, where Russia's victory turned the tide of the war.

ANALYSIS

Military experts describe the decision to invade Russia as one of Hitler's greatest mistakes. Most also believe that had Hitler followed up on his success at Dunkirk and launched an all-out invasion of Great Britain, he probably would have succeeded in forcing its surrender. Instead, he stalled until the British got back on their feet. Then he made only a halfhearted effort against them while setting his sights on Russia. Hitler left Great Britain intact, and the British eventually made him pay for that mistake.

Similarly, Germany could have won North Africa and the Mediterranean at a relatively cheap price. German forces could easily have captured Gibraltar, Suez, and Malta with just a small fraction of the effort that had been used against Russia. Then, the British ships based at Malta would not have sunk half the supplies intended for Germany's modest army in Africa. Well-supplied German armies, reinforced with aircraft wasted in the Russian campaign, could easily have controlled North Africa. If Hitler had secured the Mediterranean, Italy would not have collapsed so quickly, and the Allies would have had great difficulty trying to establish a southern front.

Hitler nearly succeeded in his gamble. Even with his monumental blunders in the Russian campaign, his armies had reached the outskirts of Moscow. Had Hitler focused completely on capturing that city, Moscow would have fallen, and the Russian army may well have disintegrated. Then he could have captured Great Britain and the Mediterranean area at his leisure.

The Germans could possibly have won the Second World War any number of ways after their victory at Dunkirk. But as it happened, Hitler's choice to invade Russia turned out to be the disaster that turned things around and spelled the beginning of the end for Germany in World War II.

3

The Imperial Japanese Navy

June 1942

Japanese forces have stormed through the Pacific Ocean since their surprise attack on the United States Navy at Pearl Harbor, Hawaii, six months ago. Their armies have overrun the Philippine Islands, Hong Kong, Singapore, and Wake Island. The Japanese navy now dominates a large area of the Pacific Ocean and has established a series of island bases that extends its control nearly halfway to the United States.

Despite Japan's advantage on the seas, its military leaders have recently been humiliated by a bombing raid, launched from American aircraft carriers, on their capital city of Tokyo. The raid has prompted a two-part Japanese mission directed at the U.S. base at Midway Island. Their first goal is to capture the base; this will extend Japan's ocean domination several hundreds of miles to the east and will make further raids on Japan almost impossible. The second, more important goal is to draw the American fleet into a battle and deal such a crippling blow that you will gain control over the Pacific for years to come.

Japanese leaders have sent a huge naval force to attack Midway Island. You are in charge of the main carrier striking force, and your group of ships includes most of Japan's aircraft carriers. These carriers will launch the planes that will bomb Midway prior to the landing of Japanese troops. With luck, the American Pacific fleet will respond to the invasion. In that case, your aircraft will attack the American ships.

The task of capturing Midway will be easier if you can achieve surprise, as Japanese forces did at Pearl Harbor. As you prepare to wave your first bombers off the carrier deck to hit Midway, you have no idea whether you will catch the Americans off guard. Nor do you have any clear idea of what American ships might be in the vicinity to challenge you.

Aboard your carriers are two main types of aircraft: There are small, fast fighters to defend both your ships and slower airplanes against attacks by enemy aircraft, and offensive planes to destroy enemy targets both on land and at sea. Your offensive planes are dive bombers and torpedo bombers. Dive bombers swoop down at high speeds on enemy targets and release bombs, which are simply explosives that detonate on impact. Bombs are most effective against land-based enemy targets, but they can damage ships as well.

Torpedo bombers are specially designed bombers that can carry either bombs or torpedoes. Torpedoes are explosives with a motor to propel them through water. They are more effective than bombs because they strike from the side and explode at or below the water line, causing ships to flood and sink. Torpedo bombers, though, are slower and easier to shoot down than dive bombers. They also need a fighter escort to protect them from enemy fighters in order to get close enough to their targets.

Although torpedo bombers can carry either bombs or torpedoes, they cannot carry both at the same time. Bombs will be more effective against the defenses at Midway Island, but torpedoes will be more effective against the American fleet. Without a sure knowledge of where the American fleet is, you are not sure how to arm your torpedo bombers.

THE OPPOSING FORCES

The Japanese raid on Pearl Harbor destroyed the powerhouses of the American fleet. Four battleships were sunk during the raid and four others were damaged. Without these heavyweight ships, the American navy cannot match the cannon power of the Japanese navy.

However, recent aviation advances have made aircraft carriers more important than battleships in naval warfare. Less than a month ago, the Americans and the Japanese fought the Battle of the Coral Sea without a single ship on either side firing a shot against an enemy ship. Aircraft from both sides carried out the attacks, sinking several ships and damaging others.

You believe that the Americans have four aircraft carriers operating in the Pacific, but one or two of these may be too crippled to see action. Your intelligence sources have been unable to locate any of these carriers recently. However, intercepted radio communications indicate that an American carrier task force may be located too far to the west to take part in the Midway action. If true, this would be good news for your landing force but would frustrate your attempts to force a decisive battle to annihilate the American fleet.

Midway Island is too small to support a large military force. No more than 2,000 American soldiers are there now, but the island is well equipped with antiaircraft guns. The Americans have recently strengthened the Midway air base so that it now has more than 100 planes. More aircraft could possibly arrive within a day from Pearl Harbor, about 1,100 miles away.

YOUR FORCES

The Japanese strike force far outnumbers the total number of American ships in the entire Pacific. You have more of every type of large ship—from aircraft carriers to battleships.

You have 20 ships in your group. The strength of this force lies in its four large aircraft carriers that carrying roughly 260 planes. About a third of these are defensive planes (fighters), and two-thirds are offensive planes (torpedo bombers and dive bombers). Your fighters have proven to be superior to the American fighters they have

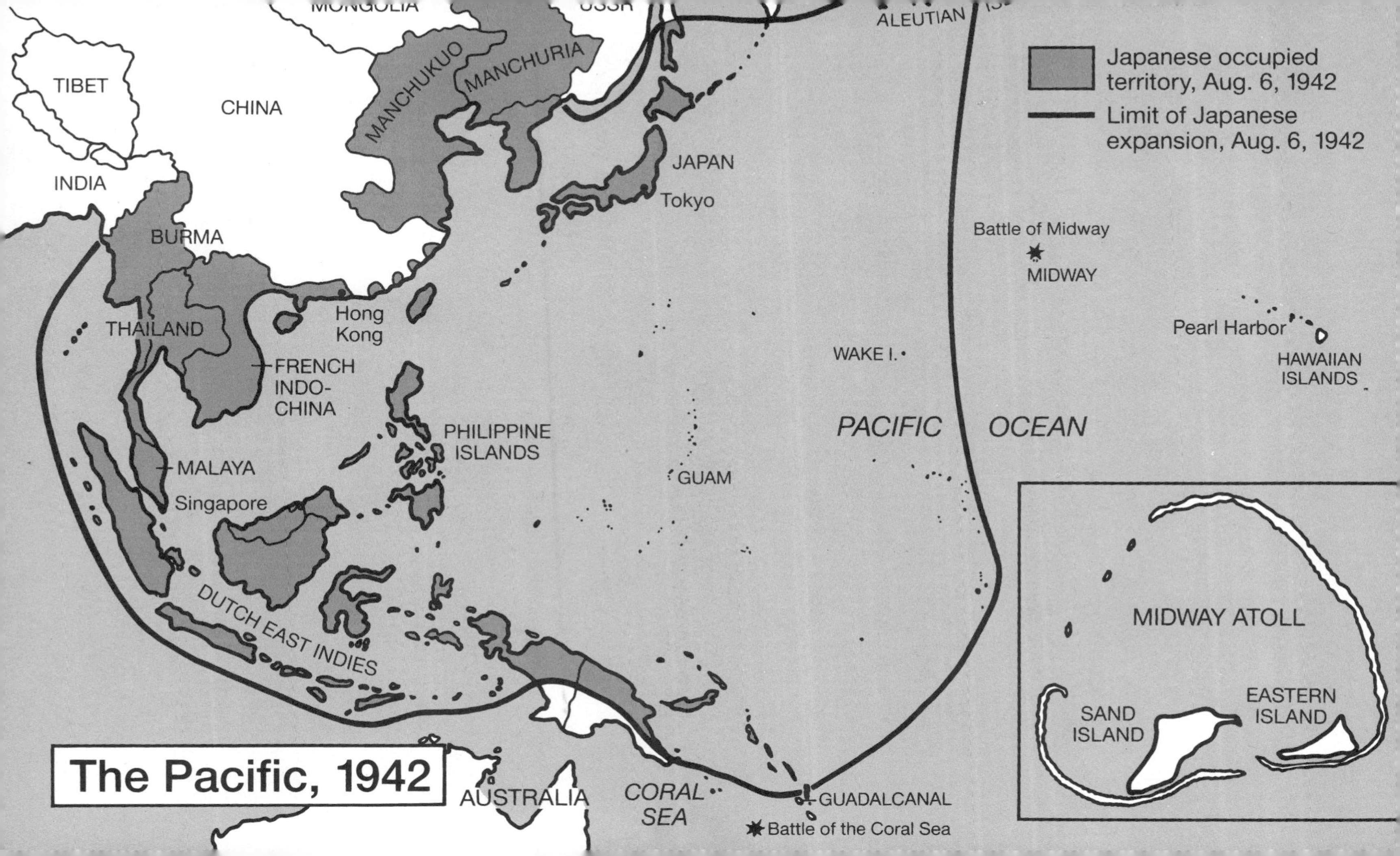

The Pacific, 1942
Japanese occupied territory, Aug. 6, 1942
Limit of Japanese expansion, Aug. 6, 1942
TIBET
CHINA
INDIA
MANCHUKUO
MANCHURIA
ALEUTIAN
JAPAN
Tokyo
BURMA
THAILAND
Hong Kong
FRENCH INDO-CHINA
MALAYA
Singapore
PHILIPPINE ISLANDS
GUAM
WAKE I.
Battle of Midway
MIDWAY
Pearl Harbor
HAWAIIAN ISLANDS
PACIFIC OCEAN
DUTCH EAST INDIES
AUSTRALIA
CORAL SEA
GUADALCANAL
Battle of the Coral Sea
MIDWAY ATOLL
SAND ISLAND
EASTERN ISLAND

encountered so far. Your offensive planes are about as effective as those flown by the Americans.

The rest of your fleet is poised several hundred miles away, ready to join the battle should the American fleet appear to fight in defense of Midway Island. Altogether, the Japanese Imperial Navy can throw 200 ships and more than 700 aircraft into battle.

YOU ARE IN COMMAND.

As you launch your scheduled predawn attack against Midway, what precautions will you take against the possibility that enemy ships are in the area?

Option 1 **Take no extra precautions.**

The Americans must defend a vast area of the Pacific Ocean with only a small number of ships. The odds that a significant force would happen to be in the area are ridiculously small. That could be possible only if the Americans have somehow broken your top-secret codes or have discovered through some freak accident that you are attacking Midway.

Your scouts and intelligence agents have not been much help in locating the Americans. But the information they have indicates that the most dangerous American ships—aircraft carriers—are far to the west.

Even when you have no reason to suspect that enemy ships are in the area, normal scouting procedure calls for you to send out a single line of patrol planes at the time you launch an attack. Each plane would search a particular section of ocean for enemy ships and then report back to command.

Given the small chance that enemy ships are near, this single line of scouts should be adequate. You should concentrate the rest of your planes against Midway to make sure you capture that island.

***Option 2* Double the number of scout planes on patrol.**

If you suspect enemies are nearby, you can gain an extra measure of safety by using a "two-phase" search. This calls for a second group of planes to search the same area as the first group after a certain interval of time. In view of the fact that you have launched your Midway attack before dawn, at a time when your first scouts will have poor visibility, this extra insurance might be wise.

Two-phase scouting has two disadvantages, however. First, it ties up seven additional planes that would then not be available for combat against either Midway or American ships. Second, in early operations in the Indian Ocean, your scout planes frequently lost track of your carriers. The carriers then had to send out signals telling the planes where to find them. The last thing you want to do is send out signals that will tell the enemy exactly where you are.

***Option 3* Hold back half of your offensive aircraft.**

While half of your bombers are attacking Midway, you can take the added safety precaution of keeping the other half on deck. Your reserve force can include both dive bombers and torpedo bombers armed with torpedoes.

This precaution would not waste aircraft on non-combat scouting duties. Should your scout planes discover enemy ships, you could instantly launch your reserve planes against these ships. A swift torpedo or dive bomber attack against enemy ships would be essential if the enemy had an aircraft carrier preparing to launch planes against you.

The glaring disadvantage of this precaution is that it would cut down the effectiveness of your attack on Midway.

THE DECISION IS YOURS. WHAT WILL YOU DO?

Option 1 **Take no extra precautions.**

Option 2 **Double the number of scout planes on patrol.**

Option 3 **Hold back half of your offensive aircraft.**

Only six months after executing the surprise attack and victory at Pearl Harbor, Japanese Admiral Chuichi Nagumo prepared to smash the U.S. naval forces at Midway.

Rear Admiral Chuichi Nagumo chose *Option 3*.

Nagumo did not believe that any American ships were patrolling the area. Yet his behavior on this assignment, according to Mitsuo Fuchida, a celebrated pilot who led Japan's raid on Pearl Harbor, was notably conservative and passive. Fuchida thought that Nagumo might have acted this way because he was trained as a torpedo warfare expert. Nagumo's superiors had assigned him to lead the carrier force because of his experience and record as an officer, but the relatively new field of aircraft carrier operations was foreign to him.

Nagumo played it safe. The Japanese fleet had overwhelming superiority, and he saw no reason to tamper with this advantage by taking chances. He held dive bombers in reserve on two aircraft carriers and torpedo bombers in reserve on the other two carriers.

RESULT

Nagumo was disappointed to learn that the Americans on Midway had been expecting an attack. When the Japanese places arrived, none of their aircraft was on the ground, and soldiers manned all battle stations. The reduced first wave of 108 Japanese planes, therefore, caused only minor damage. On his return flight to the carrier, the lead pilot radioed that another attack would be needed to finish the job.

Midway-based American torpedo bombers, meanwhile, attacked the Japanese fleet. These planes did not have a fighter escort, so they were easy prey for Japanese

An American pilot launches a torpedo over the Pacific.

fighters. The few that were not shot down caused little, if any, damage to Japanese ships.

The Japanese scout planes found no enemy fleet, so Nagumo's precaution in holding back half the aircraft in case enemy ships were discovered appeared to have been unnecessary. Certain now that no ships were nearby, Nagumo ordered the deck crew to remove the torpedoes from the torpedo bombers still on deck and to rearm these planes with bombs for a second attack on Midway.

A short while later, however, a scout plane shocked Nagumo with a report of a large American naval force of at least ten ships. Another 50 minutes passed before the scout was able to confirm that there was an aircraft carrier close by. Just as his reserve planes were being refitted with bombs for Midway, Nagumo learned that he was in danger from an unexpected American aircraft carrier.

ANALYSIS

Nagumo's caution, even when he did not suspect American ships were near, had been wise. But the option he chose proved to be unwise. The search was poorly conducted. Two of the search planes took off later than scheduled, and engine trouble forced another to turn back. The search plane flying nearest to the American force missed seeing it because of poor visibility. A second plane, returning from his search, discovered the American ships. By the time Nagumo's scout patrol located the American force, the second wave of Japanese planes was already being rearmed with bombs for land.

After learning of the American aircraft carrier, Nagumo again switched his order. He told his crew to take the bombs off the reserve torpedo planes and to put the torpedoes back on. This repeated changing of orders caused confusion and delay. Frantic to comply with orders quickly, the deck crew did not stow the bombs that they were removing safely in storage below deck. Instead, they left them for the moment on the deck. Thus, any bomb that struck the deck could set off the bombs and cause terrible explosions.

Pilot Mitsuo Fuchida believed the order to hold back half the offensive planes limited the first strike's effectiveness. He was convinced that the two-phase search ***(Option 2)*** was the proper choice. Had a second search plane covered the same area shortly after the first, the Japanese would have detected the American ships earlier. This would have spared them much confusion, and would not have left their carriers so vulnerable to attack.

On the deck of their aircraft carrier, Japanese crews ready their airplanes for combat.

NOW AN EVEN MORE URGENT DECISION FACES YOU.

Obviously, the enemy knows where you are. An attack will certainly be coming soon. Unfortunately, you now have a traffic problem. The bombers that attacked Midway Island are returning. All are low on fuel; some are damaged. Also, you sent dozens of your fighter planes into the sky to help ward off the attacks of the Midway-based American planes. Your fighters cannot stay in the air indefinitely, either.

YOU ARE IN COMMAND.

How will you proceed?

Option 1 **Recover all your planes from the air first.**

You have no reason to panic. Your force is undoubtedly far superior to the American force. Now that you have found the enemy fleet, all you need to do is stay calm, collect your planes in an orderly fashion, and regroup.

This would certainly be the best option for the planes returning from the attack on Midway. Some of them are so damaged that they cannot wait for you to launch the torpedo bombers and dive bombers now on deck. The pilots might have to ditch their planes into the sea while they wait for the decks to clear.

Furthermore, the fighters providing security for your carriers and bombers have been airborne for so long that they do not have enough fuel to escort the torpedo bombers to the American fleet. Unescorted torpedo planes are easy targets for enemy fighters. You have just witnessed what happened to American pilots who tried to attack your ships without a fighter escort. Only 3 of them even released their torpedoes. Your fighters shot down 7 of the 11.

Even the swift dive bombers, which are not as vulnerable as torpedo bombers, would suffer severe losses if they attempted an attack without a fighter escort. The smart move would be to land all of your planes, refuel the fighters that have been up in the air protecting your ships, and rearm the torpedo bombers with torpedoes. You will then send the torpedo bombers, the dive bombers, and a fighter escort to attack the American fleet.

A Japanese fighter takes off from its carrier deck.

Option 2 **Launch all reserve offensive planes immediately.**

Rear Admiral Tamon Yamaguchi, commander of the carrier *Hiryu*, has just sent a signal urging you to launch your remaining aircraft as fast as you can and send them off to strike at the enemy carrier.

Yamaguchi believes the situation is too dangerous to delay the attack. You don't know how much time you have until the American carrier aircraft attack you. If your first priority is to recover the planes in the air, you will have to stow away the aircraft that are now on the deck. However, you may need these planes sooner than you think to defend against another American attack. Better to put them into the air where they might do some good than to take them below deck where they will be worthless until the recovery is complete.

You cannot afford to have the enemy catch you with a deck load of planes as you prepare to launch an attack. Armed planes with full fuel tanks are sitting bombs. Just one hit from an American attack plane could set off a terrible chain reaction of explosions.

Even if some of the torpedo bombers are armed with bombs instead of torpedoes, you must not hesitate for a moment. Bombs may not be as effective against ships as torpedoes, but a well-placed bomb can still cause great damage.

True, you will lose most of your planes and pilots if they attack without an escort. But if an American attack finds all of your fueled and armed planes on deck, you could be facing an unthinkable catastrophe.

Option 3 **Launch dive bombers from two of the carriers and collect aircraft on the other two.**

The reserve dive bombers on the decks of the *Hiryu* and the *Soryu* are primed to attack. Crews on the *Akagi* and the *Kaga* are still refitting the reserve torpedo bombers with torpedoes.

Since the dive bombers are ready, send those out at once. After all, they are the offensive planes that have the best chance of surviving without an escort.

This option will allow you to immediately collect the returning aircraft in most urgent need of landing while getting at least some sort of strike launched without delay. It may also give your crews a chance to complete the rearming of the torpedo planes with the more effective torpedoes.

The disadvantage is that, again, your attack force against the American carrier will be only half-strength. Your strike against Midway already showed how ineffective a diluted attack can be.

THE DECISION IS YOURS.
WHAT WILL YOU DO?

Option 1 **Recover all your planes from the air first.**

Option 2 **Launch all reserve offensive planes immediately.**

Option 3 **Launch dive bombers from two of the carriers and collect aircraft on the other two.**

Admiral Nagumo chose *Option 1*.

The fresh image of unescorted American torpedo bombers bursting into flames all around his fleet must have left an impression on the cautious admiral. He decided that the risk of sending unescorted planes on a similar attack against the American fleet was too great.

Nagumo did not believe he was in immediate danger. He still had a strong squadron of fighters in the air to protect his fleet against an attack by the planes from the American carrier. Nagumo ordered recovery operations to begin.

RESULT

Twelve minutes after the Japanese carriers recovered Nagumo's last plane, aircraft from the American carrier appeared. While the Japanese fighters roared off to intercept the enemy, Japanese crews put the recovered planes below deck and prepared their reserve torpedo bombers and dive bombers for launching.

The Japanese fighters performed spectacularly, shooting down 39 of the 43 unescorted American torpedo planes. The slaughter seemed to confirm that Nagumo was correct in refusing to send his torpedo planes off the deck without fighter escort. The Japanese then completed preparations for the attack force, and Nagumo gave the order to launch.

But as the first Japanese plane lifted off the runway, American dive bombers suddenly streaked down out of the clouds. The Japanese carriers were utterly helpless.

Their decks were crammed with armed and fueled planes. In the air, the Japanese fighter planes—pulled out of position by their fight with the torpedo plane attack—could only watch.

Explosions and searing flames swept over three of the carriers. The fuel tanks, bombs, and torpedoes of the Japanese planes blew up, feeding the infernos until they were out of control. Within minutes, the *Kaga*, *Soryu*, and *Akagi* were destroyed along with all of their aircraft, and most of their pilots perished in the flames.

The *Hiryu* survived and was able to launch attacks the next day that destroyed the American aircraft carrier *Yorktown*. But, in turn, another wave of American aircraft sunk the *Hiryu*.

ANALYSIS

Not until the second day of the attack did the Japanese realize they were dealing with not one but three American aircraft carriers. The Americans had broken the Japanese top-secret code and had a good idea what the Japanese fleet was planning to do. (They had only intercepted parts of the Japanese plans but knew Midway was the target.) American carriers lay in ambush on the eastern side of Midway Island. As the Japanese planes flew to Midway for their attack, aircraft from the American carriers took off in full force to attack the Japanese fleet.

Fuchida saw immediately that Nagumo's decision was a mistake. The pilot noted that speed is as important as strength in a military engagement. At the least, he thought that Nagumo should have sent the dive bombers

Badly damaged by Japanese aircraft on June 4, 1942, the USS Yorktown, *here in flames, sank three days later.*

out at once. He could even have launched the torpedo bombers and have ordered them to circle in the air long enough for a few fighters to land, refuel, and join them for an escort. If time did not permit that, Fuchida believed that Nagumo should have sent the torpedo bombers on the attack without escort. Fuchida believed that the risk "should have been accepted as necessary in this emergency." The damaged Japanese planes returning from Midway could have crash-landed in the sea if they were unable to wait for the decks to clear. Nagumo's ships could have easily rescued the pilots from the sea.

According to Fuchida, even the direct hits taken by the big carriers should not have been enough to disable them. But the chain of explosions caused by the fuel tanks, bombs, and torpedoes of the unlaunched aircraft

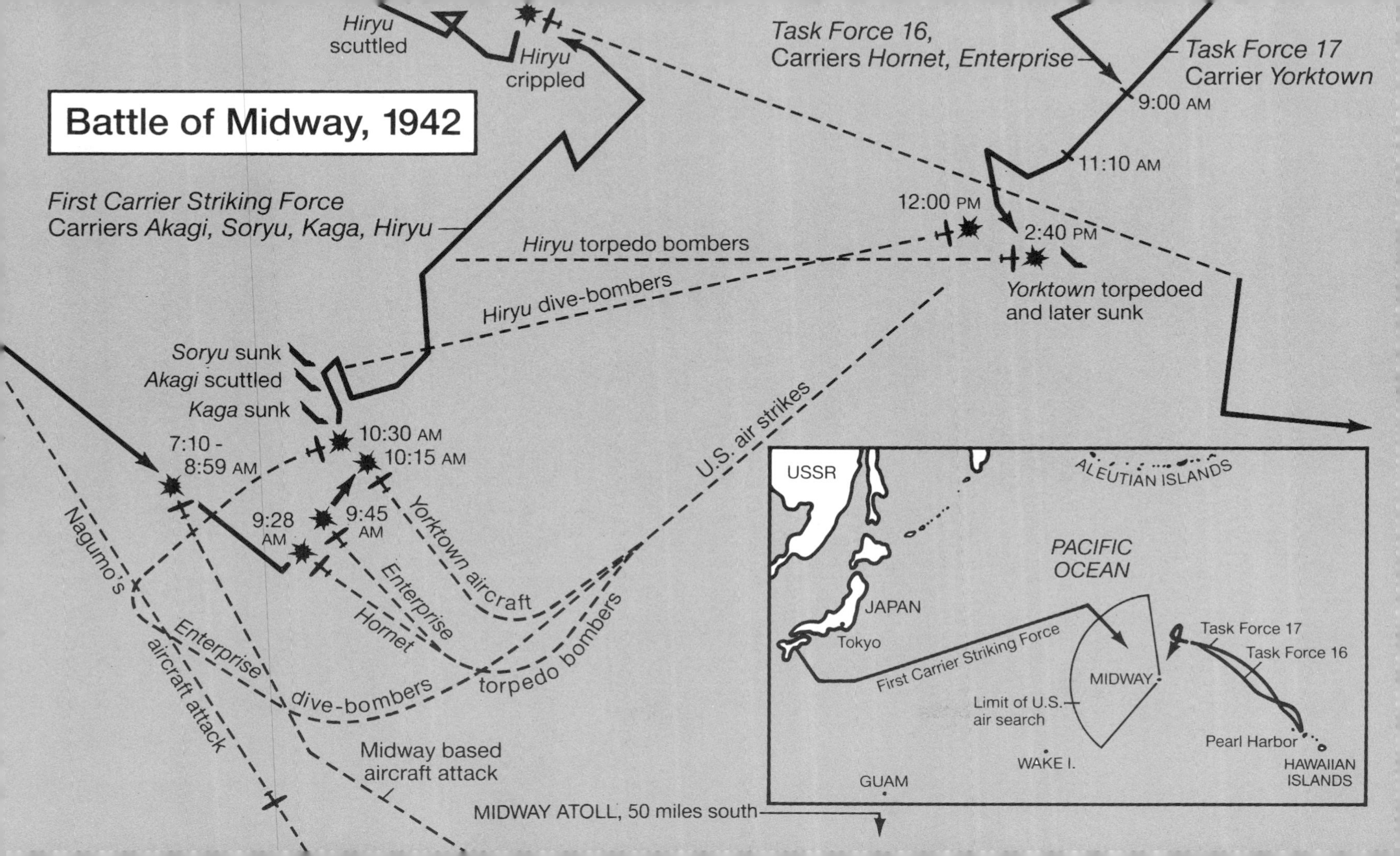
Battle of Midway, 1942
Hiryu scuttled
Hiryu crippled
Task Force 16,
Carriers Hornet, Enterprise
Task Force 17
Carrier Yorktown
9:00 AM
11:10 AM
12:00 PM
2:40 PM
First Carrier Striking Force
Carriers Akagi, Soryu, Kaga, Hiryu
Hiryu torpedo bombers
Hiryu dive-bombers
Yorktown torpedoed and later sunk
Soryu sunk
Akagi scuttled
Kaga sunk
7:10 - 8:59 AM
10:30 AM
10:15 AM
9:28 AM
9:45 AM
U.S. air strikes
Yorktown aircraft
Enterprise
Hornet
torpedo bombers
dive-bombers
Nagumo's
Enterprise aircraft attack
Midway based aircraft attack
MIDWAY ATOLL, 50 miles south
USSR
ALEUTIAN ISLANDS
PACIFIC OCEAN
JAPAN
Tokyo
First Carrier Striking Force
MIDWAY
Limit of U.S. air search
Task Force 17
Task Force 16
Pearl Harbor
HAWAIIAN ISLANDS
WAKE I.
GUAM

had sealed their fate. Had these aircraft taken off, the carriers might well have survived the attack.

Nagumo's decisions caused a far superior Japanese navy to suffer a decisive defeat at the hands of its weaker foe. Japan lost 4 large aircraft carriers, more than 250 aircraft, and many of its best pilots at the Battle of Midway Island.

The defeat so weakened the Japanese navy that it was never again able to take offensive actions in the Pacific Ocean. The disaster at Midway forced Japan to abandon its plans to isolate Australia and extend its control as far as Hawaii. Three months later, the Americans were free to take their first offensive action of the war at Guadalcanal. From that point on, Japan retreated from its newly conquered lands until it finally surrendered to the United States on September 2, 1945.

4

The Allied Forces
June 1944

Great Britain has survived the bombing attacks of its German enemies and is no longer threatened with extinction. Losses in the Soviet Union and the Mediterranean Sea have taken a heavy toll on a German military machine that once seemed invincible.

But the Germans are far from defeated. They still control virtually the entire continent of Europe. The Russians, fighting furiously against the Germans on the eastern front, are begging for a western offensive so that they do not have to keep bearing the brunt of the German firepower.

For many months, American and British forces in Great Britain have been planning Operation Overlord for just that purpose. The plan calls for Allied troops to cross the English Channel and attack the Nazi-occupied

Britain's Royal Air Force (RAF) contributed greatly to keeping the Nazis off British soil. Here an RAF Spitfire *in aerial combat flies beneath a German bomber.*

province of Normandy in northwestern France. This will be one of the most ambitious and dangerous enterprises of the war. The invasion troops will be exposed to enemy fire as landing craft transport them across the water and onto open beaches strewn with land mines. Paratroopers, who will be dropped behind enemy lines to capture key locations, will run a harrowing risk of being shot out of the sky. Unless your soldiers carry out every phase of the complex invasion plan, this could be the worst military catastrophe in modern history.

Your staff has pinpointed the exact conditions that will give you the greatest chance of success against the German coastal defenses. You would prefer transporting your troops across the channel at night to avoid attacks from German aircraft. The pilots of the transport planes and gliders will need moonlight in order to see their landing targets, and the paratroopers can only jump in mild winds. The landing craft should arrive at Normandy one hour after daylight to allow the Allied navy and air forces a chance to bombard the German defenses on the beaches. Ideally, the landing would be made 30 minutes after low tide, when the water depth will allow the engineers to blast a path through the mine fields. To reduce the risk of landing craft swamping in rough seas and for smooth landings on the beaches, the waves must be no more than three or four feet high. For the air force to do its job effectively, the cloud cover must be no lower than 3,000 feet.

The moon and tides will be favorable on June 6, then not again until June 19. Favorable weather, however, is not so predictable. Bad weather could disrupt your entire timetable. You must weigh all of these factors in deciding when you will begin the invasion.

THE OPPOSING FORCES

The Germans have been expecting a cross-channel attack for some time, so an invasion will not catch them by surprise.

Germany currently has 58 army divisions in western Europe; 10 of them are armored divisions. Although this is a sizable and effective fighting force, these divisions must defend over 3,000 miles of coastline. Therefore, they are generally spread quite thin. The Germans have placed their strongest defenses at Pas de Calais, the narrowest point of the channel where the crossing would be the easiest.

That does not mean, however, that the Germans have neglected the Normandy defenses. Some German officers have suspected that Normandy might be your objective, and coastal defenses there are second only to those at Pas de Calais. To keep ships at bay, huge guns guard the Normandy beaches, which the Germans have strewn with mines. Up to eight German divisions will be stationed in the vicinity to fight off the initial landing, and Germany can reinforce these divisions within 48 hours.

Germany's weak navy will not be a factor in preventing the invasion. Moreover, the air war over Great Britain and in other war sectors has badly depleted Germany's air force, so its effectiveness against the invasion will be limited.

A German soldier peers out to the English Channel from his steel and concrete gun emplacement on the coast of France.

YOUR FORCES

Your initial landing forces will roughly equal the German defenders in the Normandy region. This includes 23,000 airborne troops and about 130,000 who will land on the beaches. However, to ensure success, the assaulting force should ideally outnumber the well-entrenched defenders.

You hope to make up for this weakness with your air force. You have nearly 6,000 bombers ready to attack enemy positions and more than 5,000 fighter planes to protect the bombers. This should give your forces complete control of the skies. Your navy will add its heavy guns in support of the landing.

The trickiest part of Operation Overlord will be coordinating the entire effort. More than 4,000 landing craft will be crossing the English Channel in the dark and attacking five different beaches. Your soldiers must establish a firm hold on the beaches and then link up with airborne troops dropped at various locations. Everything must be done quickly before the German defenders gather enough reinforcements to push you off the beaches.

Once you get established on the beaches and forge into enemy territory, you can begin to bring in reinforcements. You have 39 Allied divisions stationed in southern England. It will take three weeks, however, to ferry all of them across the channel.

YOU ARE IN COMMAND.

The early morning sky on June 5 is overcast, and winds are whipping around at near gale force. If your assault forces are to reach Normandy at dawn on June 6, they must leave now. You must decide when to attack.

Option 1 **Order the attack for dawn on June 6, as scheduled.**

Field Marshal Bernard Montgomery, the commander of the British ground forces for Operation Overlord, advises you to get going. Your chief meteorologist, John Stagg, detects a high pressure area off to the northwest, sandwiched between two storms. He is predicting that this will bring a break in the bad weather very soon. His best guess is that a weak weather system might give you as long as 36 hours of acceptable conditions for your troops to establish themselves on the coast of Normandy before the next storm arrives.

Admittedly, relying on this forecast involves a risk. But this spring you already postponed the invasion from May until June in order to gather more landing craft. Yesterday, stormy weather forced you to call another 24-hour postponement. Some of your troops have been cooped up in their sea transports for as long as 72 hours. This on-again, off-again indecision is emotionally draining. Another postponement now would be the worst thing for the morale of your troops.

Furthermore, every day of delay gives the Germans more opportunity to strengthen their unfinished coastal defenses and to bring in reinforcements. Every day of

Allied army commanders at Normandy (from left): British Field Marshal Bernard Montgomery, and American generals Dwight Eisenhower and Omar Bradley

delay also increases the risk that the Germans will learn more details about the coming invasion.

Option 2 **Postpone the attack until dawn on June 19.**

This is the next time that the moon and the tides will be most favorable for the invasion. Far better to put off the attack for two weeks than risk such an important action on what one of your own generals calls a "chancy" weather report.

The problem with the forecast is that your meteorologists have been disagreeing all week. This is one of the strangest weather patterns Great Britain has ever seen. Even Stagg admits that he went back over weather charts for the past 40 to 50 years without finding a summertime pattern similar to this. Early yesterday, no one on the five-person meteorological staff agreed on the forecast for the next 24 hours.

The invasion depends absolutely on good weather conditions. If your aircraft cannot get up into the sky to provide strong support, the Germans will shoot your ground forces to pieces. If your troops cross the sea in waters so choppy that they get seasick and can't fight, the whole enterprise will end in disaster. Even the most optimistic forecast predicts only moderately good conditions for parachuting. If the winds pick up more than predicted, the paratroopers cannot jump. General Omar Bradley, who commands the American landing group for Operation Overlord, says he will not send his troops to the beaches without paratrooper support.

Option 3 **Order the invasion on June 8 or 9 at midday.**

There are two problems with waiting for a night attack on June 19. First, if the weather at that time is no better than now, or even worse, you would have to postpone the invasion yet another time. How long can you hold your troops in readiness?

Also, time is already beginning to run out. Allied leaders were hoping to break out from the beaches with a strong offensive that would hurl the Germans back to their own borders. But the best time for fighting an offensive is during warm weather. You have already lost the month of May. By postponing further, you could be squandering June.

The German forces in the west are formidable. Even if you land successfully at Normandy, you will not gain ground against them easily. By postponing your invasion until July, you leave your armies precious little time to establish your offensive before winter comes. If you expect to launch it at all this year, you cannot afford to postpone this invasion much longer.

American military leaders have been urging this invasion since 1942. The war-ravaged civilians of Europe who are being held captive in the grip of the Nazi regime are desperate for relief. Furthermore, the Allies have assured the battered Russian army that they will establish a western front soon. To retain the trust of your Allies, you must carry through on that promise.

Although the navy argues strongly that the invasion must sail at night and attack at dawn, some of your most trusted generals, such as Omar Bradley and Leonard Gerow, do not agree. Bradley believes that "an overdose of daylight had become . . . preferable to the ordeal of a long delay." Darkness and moonlight and the right tides would be nice, but by far the most important element of your attack is air support. Rather than take chances with the weather, you should go for the conditions that facilitate the best flying conditions and take your chances with the rest. Your air force and navy are so strong that they could cover the assault with a devastating curtain of fire. A daylight assault would also reduce the chances that some troops would miss the landing targets.

Option 4 **Postpone the invasion until 1945.**

This type of operation is so risky that you dare not attempt it unless you can be certain of ideal conditions. No weather forecaster can give you any assurance that the weather will be perfect in the next few weeks. Therefore, you had best postpone Operation Overlord.

An impatient or hurried attempt to carry out the invasion would play right into the Germans' hands. The Germans have stationed a third of their fighting forces in western Europe to guard against the possibility of an attack from Great Britain. As long as the nearly 3 million Allied troops remain in Great Britain, Germany's weak air force and navy cannot do much to them.

But once these Allied forces leave that island and set foot on the mainland, the powerful German army will have a chance to attack them and gain the victory its dispirited soldiers so badly need. Great Britain is sending its last reserves of troops into the invasion. If the Germans can thwart the assault, they will have destroyed the threat from the west, probably for many years to come. With their western borders secure, Germany could then transfer 50 divisions to the Russian or Italian fronts. These new troops, confident after their victory in the west, could turn the tide of battle.

A premature Operation Overlord could give Germany the victory it needs to regain its strength. The Allies' track record for cross-channel attacks is grim. In the summer of 1942, a small-scale raid at Dieppe on the French coast proved to be an utter failure.

Sir Trafford Leigh-Mallory, the commander of the Allied air forces for Operation Overlord, has so little

Sir Trafford Leigh-Mallory, chief of Britain's air forces, took a grim view of the invasion's chances for success.

confidence in the invasion plans that he has issued a written protest against them. Leigh-Mallory predicts that your paratroopers will suffer casualties as high as 70 percent and that up to half of them will die before they hit the ground. He says that if your success depends on paratroopers, the entire plan is unsafe even in ideal conditions.

One of your closest aides, General Bedell Smith, believes your troops will be able to seize the beach, but he worries about a German counterattack. Within a week or two of the initial landing, the German reinforcements will outnumber the Allied invaders. Smith puts the odds of success for Operation Overlord at fifty-fifty.

To make matters worse, just a week ago the Germans moved a division of soldiers to Omaha Beach, one of the two landing beaches in Normandy targeted by the American forces. You no longer have time to change your plans for the attack. If you invade Europe this year, the soldiers who come ashore at Omaha Beach will be facing greater forces than you had anticipated.

The reasonable course of action is to postpone the invasion for a year. That ties up German troops, who must remain on guard in the west. If the Russians squawk about your promise for a second front to relieve the pressure against them, you can point to the American invasion of Italy. That certainly is a second front and is tying up German forces there. Perhaps by next spring those Allied forces in Italy will have advanced far enough into Europe that the Germans will have to take some divisions away from their Atlantic defenses. That will give your Normandy invasion a better chance to succeed.

THE DECISION IS YOURS.
WHAT WILL YOU DO?

Option 1 **Order the attack for dawn on June 6, as scheduled.**

Option 2 **Postpone the attack until dawn on June 19.**

Option 3 **Order the invasion on June 8 or 9 at midday.**

Option 4 **Postpone the invasion until 1945.**

Allied soldiers approach the Normandy beaches.

General Dwight Eisenhower felt the awesome responsibility of organizing and commanding the combined U.S. and British air, land, and sea forces that would invade German-occupied France.

General Dwight Eisenhower decided on *Option 1.*

Eisenhower rarely slept in the weeks before setting Operation Overlord in motion. The uncertain weather and Leigh-Mallory's concerns about the paratroopers only added to the weight of responsibility he bore as supreme commander of the Normandy invasion. At one point, he was heard to complain that "the weather in this country is practically unpredictable."

After a fitful sleep on the night of June 4, Eisenhower concluded that delaying the invasion further would be disastrous. He was especially concerned about the possibility of a letdown in his troops' morale and the chance that Germany would use the time to continue to strengthen its coastal defenses in France.

Eisenhower discussed the matter one last time with his staff. Then he decided to stake everything on Stagg's weather prediction. "Okay, let's go," he said. While the invasion force was crossing the channel, an anxious Eisenhower made clear that he expected to shoulder the entire blame if the expedition should end in disaster. "My decision to attack at this time and place was based upon the best information available," he wrote. "If any blame attaches to this attempt, it is mine alone."

RESULT

As Stagg had predicted, the weather cleared long enough for the troops to cross the channel and attack the beaches, supported by a thundering display of naval bombardment. Flying conditions were adequate for the Allies to fly more than 10,000 missions (in contrast to only 319 by the German air force). These flights pinned down the defenders and blocked German reinforcements from arriving. Contrary to fears, the airborne casualties were light, and the air troops contributed greatly to the success of the operation. With the exception of a hard-fought victory on Omaha Beach, the Allies captured all of their targeted beaches with relative ease. By the end of the first day of fighting, the Allies had gained a beachhead 15 miles long and 2 miles wide on the European continent at a relatively light cost of 2,500 casualties.

The Germans attempted to counterattack. But the skies were so thick with Allied bombers in the first few days of the attack that the German reserves did not dare venture out from under cover until after dark. The Allies solidified their gains and in little more than three months broke out from their enclave on the French coast and drove the Germans back toward their border.

Soldiers and supplies continued to flow from Great Britain to the Allied forces in France. Now Germany was boxed in and was forced to defend against attacks from three sides: France on the west, Italy on the south, and Russia on the east. The three-front war steadily sapped Germany's strength. On May 7, 1945, Germany surrendered to the Allied forces.

An aerial view of Normandy on D-Day, the day the Allies invaded Nazi-occupied France

ANALYSIS

Winston Churchill called Operation Overlord "the most difficult and complicated operation that has ever taken place." Eisenhower's decision to launch the attack despite the unsettled weather conditions was the key to its success.

German meteorologists alerted the German defense forces every day as to the probability, based on the weather, of an Allied invasion. On the morning of June 5, the German command concluded that the weather was so awful that the Allies would be unable to mount an invasion in the coming days. Unable to detect the brief clearing that was coming, the forecasters predicted several more days of bad weather. The Germans were so convinced that an invasion was impossible that their coastal commanders left their posts to attend meetings hundreds of miles away. The arrival of the invasion force on the morning of June 6 caught them completely by surprise and was largely responsible for the astounding success of the all-important first waves of the assault.

A daylight attack on June 8 or 9 would not have achieved this surprise. Had Eisenhower played it safe and waited until favorable night conditions on June 19, the result could have been a fiasco. On that night, a severe storm lashed the French coast. With the fighting season growing shorter, Eisenhower would have been tempted to take a chance and launch the June 19 attack rather than wait another year. Had he underestimated the storm, he might have launched the invasion into the teeth of what one observer called "the worst weather

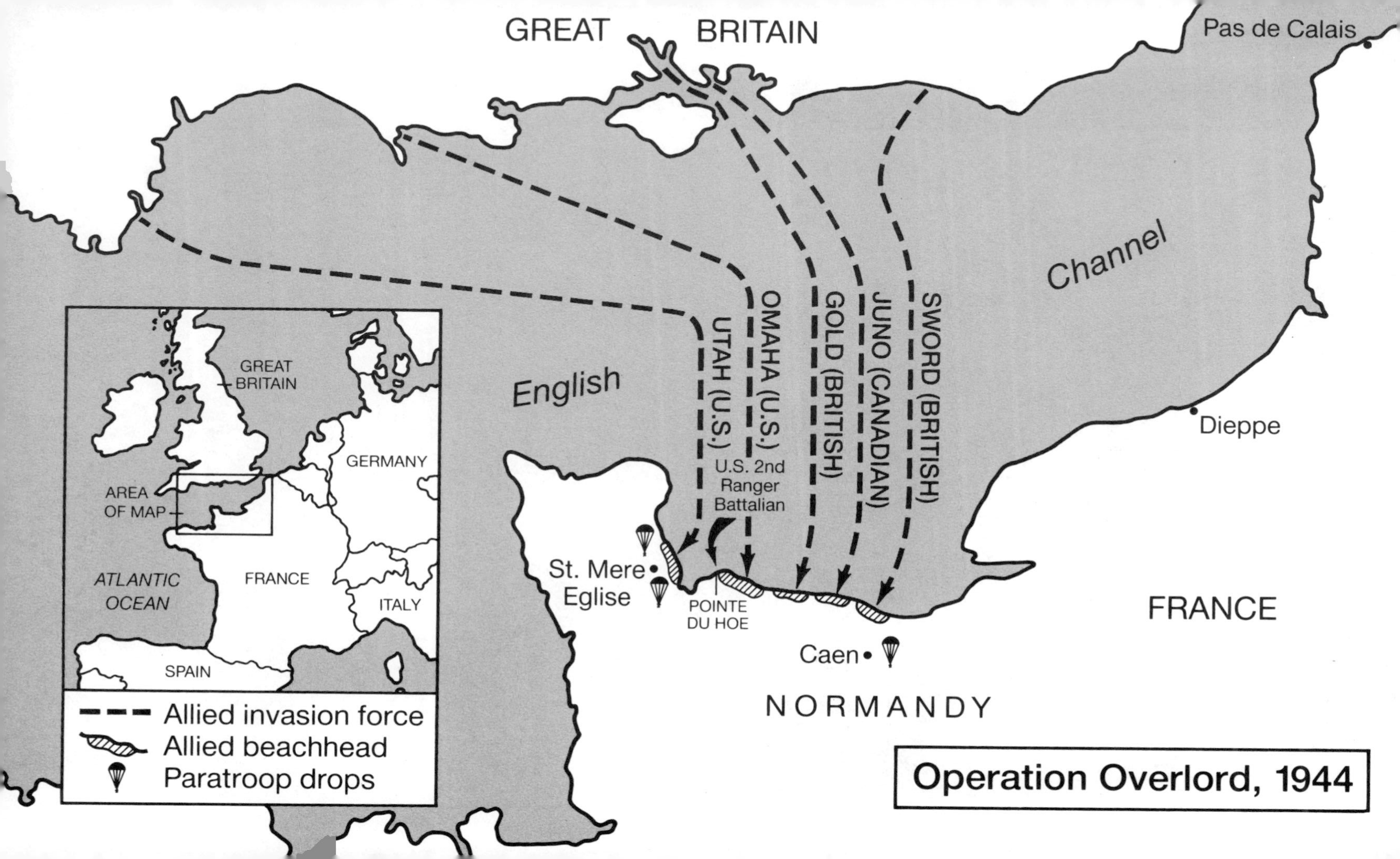

Operation Overlord, 1944

General Eisenhower addresses his paratroopers, important contributors to Operation Overlord's success.

encountered in the channel in 20 years." Any invasion launched then would have ended tragically.

More likely, Eisenhower would have postponed Operation Overlord until July. Since it rained during most of July that year, the invasion might well have been called off until the following year. Any decision that postponed the invasion for a year would have, at best, prolonged the war unnecessarily.

For all of these reasons, one of Eisenhower's adversaries, German Vice-Admiral Friedrich Ruge, described the decision to order the invasion on June 6 as "one of the truly great decisions in military history."

5

The Forces of the United Nations

July 1950

The Korean peninsula extends about 600 miles into the Pacific Ocean between the Yellow Sea and the Sea of Japan. The land has been conquered a number of times, most recently in 1910 by the Japanese. When the Japanese Empire collapsed at the end of World War II, the United States temporarily occupied the southern portion of the peninsula, while the Soviets occupied the northern part.

Attempts to unite the country were doomed because of the competing philosophies of the superpowers. The Communists took over North Korea, while South Korea worked toward a form of democracy. Tension between the two sides occasionally ran high. Leaders of both sides wanted a united Korea under their form of government.

Yet most of the world was caught by surprise when the North Koreans launched a furious invasion on June 25, 1950. Supported by dozens of tanks, their powerful army overwhelmed the border forces of South Korea. Scattering all resistance, the North Koreans captured the South Korean capital of Seoul within a few days.

The United Nations condemned the North Korean aggression and voted to send armed forces to stop the invasion. As the most powerful nation in the non-Communist world, the United States shouldered the main burden of the effort.

What followed was a race to reinforce South Korea before the North Koreans could capture the entire country. Unfortunately, the United States and its allies are losing that race. The units they have sent to Korea have been unable to stop the relentless advance of the North Koreans, who have now pushed 200 miles beyond the South Korean border.

Now, in late July, your forces are teetering on the edge of disaster. They have been boxed into a small corner of the peninsula near the city of Pusan. The top command back in Washington, D.C., has ruled out the use of nuclear weapons for fear of the conflict escalating into a nuclear war with North Korea's allies, the Russians.

THE OPPOSING FORCES

North Korea's population is only about 9 million, compared to the 21 million of South Korea. But the north is more industrially developed than the largely agricultural south.

Accurate information about the strength of the North Korean army is difficult to obtain so early in the fighting. The best guess is that somewhere around 100,000 soldiers are closing in on the perimeter around Pusan. They have demonstrated that they are well trained, ably commanded, and equipped with a large number of top-quality, Russian-made tanks.

Your intelligence sources also estimate that North Korea has posted about 6,500 soldiers in the area of Seoul and has scattered pockets of soldiers in other areas.

At the start of the war, North Korea had 180 Russian-made combat aircraft. American fighters and bombers have already destroyed most of these. The North Koreans have no navy to speak of.

Roads in South Korea are few and poorly maintained. The North Korean attack forces are being supplied by a single main corridor that runs down the length of the country from Seoul, which lies near the North Korean border. North Korean forces have reacted to frequent air strikes against this supply line by using the road almost exclusively at night.

YOUR FORCES

The South Korean soldiers are tough fighters but have taken a terrible beating from the larger, better-equipped North Korean army. Their fighting units have been beaten so badly that fewer than 50,000 South Korean soldiers are available to defend the Pusan enclave.

Troops sent by the United States and 16 other countries under the banner of the United Nations bring the total of armed forces to roughly 180,000—about the same number as the enemy. Most of these soldiers, however, are inexperienced and unprepared. The United States government has largely neglected its military since World War II. An inadequate supply of weapons, vehicles, and other equipment has hampered the efforts of the American army in Korea. Only recently have your troops been supplied with any weapons that could stop the North Korean tanks, and ammunition for these weapons is low. Finding themselves constantly outgunned and outflanked—and occasionally surrounded—some of these American and U.N. troops have become overly cautious. In recent days, they have been retreating even before the enemy has made contact with them.

The air force of the United States is unmatched and has gained control of the skies. The Americans had hoped this air superiority would be enough to stem the North Korean advance. But except for disrupting supply lines and eliminating the North Korean air force, the bombing has done little to slow the enemy advance.

More than 200 vessels of the United States Navy control the waters around Korea. This gives the U.N. and South Korean forces an open supply line from the outside and also offers support bombardment near the coast.

YOU ARE IN COMMAND.

Your army has its back to the sea at Pusan and has no more room to run. What will you do to salvage the situation and repel the invasion?

U.S. soldiers pass a destroyed Russian-built tank of the North Korean army.

Option 1 **Land an invasion force far behind enemy lines at Inchon.**

North Korea's long, thin supply line presents a tempting target. If you could cut off that supply line, the North Koreans would be unable to sustain their offensive for long.

The supply line runs through Seoul, which lies just 18 miles to the east of the port city of Inchon. An attack at Inchon would be risky because that location is some 200 miles behind the present enemy lines. But one principle of war states that the further behind enemy lines you can strike, the more profound the effect—assuming you can pull off the attack.

A bold move to seize Inchon and Seoul in one quick step could cut North Korea's supply lines, break the momentum of their attack, and devastate their morale.

The North Koreans around Pusan would then have to watch their backside for fear of being cut off and encircled by the American troops moving down from Inchon. They would either retreat or, at the very least, divert some of their troops from the offensive to take care of the invasion force.

While this option offers the greatest chance for spectacular success, it also presents the greatest chance for devastating failure. Inchon happens to be one of the most difficult harbors in the world to attack. One Navy officer reports, "We drew up a list of every conceivable and natural handicap and Inchon had 'em all."

Some of the highest tides in the world lap the Inchon shoreline. The difference between the sea level at high and low tides is 32 feet. At low tide, the landing area is a mudflat that stretches three miles into the sea, keeping ships too far away to provide support. Even at high tide, the strong current running in and out of the narrow channels poses a navigational nightmare.

More problems stand in the way of a successful invasion. The harbor is split by a small island. A small defensive force positioned on that island could train a murderous fire on any landing effort. You will need to take control of that island before you can land troops on the beach. Because of the strange tides, an invasion would require naval bombardment and an attempted landing on the island during the first tide. Then you could send troops ashore on the second tide. These maneuvers would strand your troops for 12 hours on the island as they wait for the tides to change.

One final problem exists. Inchon presents no flat landing beaches. Marines would have to storm over a sea wall right into the city. The North Koreans, of course, are well aware of these difficulties. Taking into account all of the obstacles, they probably assume that Inchon is the last place you would ever try to attack. Should you be fortunate and skilled enough to overcome these obstacles, you would certainly have the advantage of surprise.

***Option 2* Land an invasion force a short ways behind enemy lines at Kunsan.**

Most of the strategists in your army favor some kind of landing behind enemy lines. By opening a new battle front, you would relieve some of the pressure from the ring that is tightening around Pusan.

But virtually all high ranking officers in your army prefer to see the attempt made closer to the current battle front. The North Koreans cannot begin to guard the more than 5,600 miles of jagged coastline of Korea, so there is a good chance you can get in somewhere with little opposition. Kunsan, a western port 100 miles south of Inchon, would be an ideal landing place. It lies behind enemy lines yet within reach of your army at Pusan.

General J. Lawton Collins, chief of staff of the U.S. Army, points out that by getting too far behind enemy lines, you run the risk of getting trapped there. The only way to prevent a landing force from being isolated and wiped out is for it to link up as quickly as possible with your main invasion force. By placing your assault so far behind the front lines, an Inchon landing puts too great a distance between the two sections of your army and makes the task of a quick linkup extremely hazardous.

The consequences of failure at Inchon are enormous. If the marines should fail to gain the beach or if they should get pinned down and unable to break out of their beachhead, your army is finished. You will have accomplished nothing but a weakening of your already precarious position around Pusan. Your forces appear to be so close to defeat right now that such a failure would finish them off.

Kunsan, on the other hand, presents many of the advantages of the Inchon attack and is within easier reach of your trapped and exhausted army huddled around Pusan. Moreover, Kunsan does not present quite the tangle of natural obstacles that you find at Inchon. Nor are there likely to be as many North Korean soldiers in the region as are near Inchon.

***Option 3* Concentrate all your forces around the Pusan perimeter.**

The amphibious assault (land forces attacking from the sea) proposed for Inchon or Kunsan would take away troops that you desperately need at Pusan. If the assault fails, your army will be defeated. Your weakened forces at Pusan would probably not be able to fight off further attacks from the North Koreans.

Many experts believe that no type of amphibious assault is worth the risk in this modern age. Military historians will never forget the famous disaster at Gallipoli in World War I, in which a tiny force of Turks armed with machine guns obliterated a British amphibian invasion force. Even though amphibious assaults were used effectively in the Pacific island campaigns of World War II, many experts believe their high risk in the face of modern firepower makes them a thing of the past. U.S. General Omar Bradley, chairman of the Joint Chiefs of Staff, has so little faith in this tactic that he has predicted the world will never see another large-scale amphibious assault.

Even if you thought an amphibious assault was a good option, this is a poor time to try it because the country is the middle of the typhoon season. Amphibious landings require precise execution, which would be impossible if one of these Pacific storms should strike while the campaign is in progress.

Rather than gamble with the lives of 100,000 soldiers, you should pour all of your strength into the Pusan defense. Time is on your side in this war. More soldiers and weapons are arriving from the United States and from the United Nations every week. Meanwhile, the North Koreans are at the end of a long, thin supply line that is under frequent attack. Their impressive successes were gained only at the price of severe casualties. They are not likely to get more troops to replace the casualties they have suffered.

The North Koreans cannot hope to match the military strength of the United Nations forces once they are all in place. Their only chance of winning the war is to end it quickly. By taking a chance on amphibious assaults, you would give the North Koreans that chance. At all costs, you must avoid decisive engagements and hold on to your defensive position until the war turns in your favor.

There are some indications that the momentum of the war has already changed. Some people suspect that the North Koreans are already weaker than your reports estimate. Also, the further they advance toward Pusan, the closer the North Koreans come to the sea where they draw within range of your big naval guns. As long as you concentrate all your forces around Pusan, the enemy will not be able to finish you off.

Option 4 **Evacuate all forces from Pusan and leave Korea to the Communists.**

The United Nations forces on the Pusan perimeter have been suffering an average of 1,000 casualties a day. They have endured a harrowing month of fighting in which the enemy has beaten them at nearly every turn. The North Koreans have shoved the U.N. forces back through the length of South Korea into a small corner of only 50 square miles. Thus, the North Koreans have left you little room for maneuvering.

Some advisers believe that your forces are so demoralized that they may never be an effective fighting force. If that is true, they will not be able to break out of Pusan and link up with an invasion force, whether at Inchon or at Kunsan. They may not be able to hold together even if you concentrate all your forces in the Pusan corner.

If they cannot fight off the North Koreans, you could be responsible for a bloodbath. You have heard stories of the terrible treatment American prisoners suffer at the hands of the North Koreans. General Walton Walker, commander of the American forces around Pusan, does not mince words. He says the collapse of your forces "would result in one of the greatest butcheries in history."

The location of Korea makes it, at best, a doubtful proposition for the U.S. military. Korea is halfway around the world from the United States. North Korea shares a common border with both giants of the Communist

U.S. generals Douglas MacArthur and Walton Walker (right) faced bleak choices for rallying United Nations forces in Korea.

world—China and Russia. Trying to defeat the Communists in their own back yard is hopeless. The best thing to do is admit defeat, leave Korea, and get your troops safely away as best you can.

THE DECISION IS YOURS. WHAT WILL YOU DO?

Option 1 **Land an invasion force far behind enemy lines at Inchon.**

Option 2 **Land an invasion force a short ways behind enemy lines at Kunsan.**

Option 3 **Concentrate all your forces around the Pusan perimeter.**

Option 4 **Evacuate all forces from Pusan and leave Korea to the Communists.**

The Korean War capped General Douglas MacArthur's brilliant military career, one of the most distinguished in U.S. history.

General Douglas MacArthur chose *Option 1*.

Virtually every other authority in the U.S. military opposed the Inchon landing. It was MacArthur's idea, first hatched while he observed the fall of Seoul to the North Koreans in June. MacArthur was undoubtedly the only military commander in the world who could have made that choice and persuaded superiors to let him try it. The 71-year-old general enjoyed a towering reputation as hero of the war in the Pacific, and he had an ego to match his reputation. "I realize that Inchon is a 5,000-to-1 gamble, but I am used to taking such odds," he boasted at one point.

That was an exaggeration. MacArthur had sound reasons for such a daring landing at Inchon. He had used bold amphibious tactics time and time again during World War II with spectacular success. On one occasion, he had landed a force 500 miles up the New Guinea coast from the battle front, putting enemy troops in such a bad military position that they surrendered without a fight.

MacArthur believed he could use the hazards and obstacles of the Inchon landing to his advantage. "The impracticalities involved will tend to ensure for me the element of surprise," he explained.

The general decided the landing was worth the risk because, if successful, it would completely turn the tables on the North Koreans. It could end the conflict quickly and avoid a long, drawn-out war. By forcing the North Korean offensive to collapse completely, MacArthur believed he could be saving 100,000 lives that would be lost in a brutal massacre along the Pusan perimeter. "We shall land at Inchon and I shall crush them," he declared.

RESULT

The United States began bombarding Inchon by air and sea on September 10, 1950. Its forces shelled and bombed numerous other targets at the same time so as not to give away its intentions at Inchon.

On September 15, U.S. marines landed on the small island of Wolmi-do in the Inchon harbor. Resistance from the North Koreans was light, and U.S. forces secured the island after a five-and-a-half-hour fight. The group maintained its position for seven and a half hours until more marines landed at two points on the coast. Scaling the sea wall with ladders, the attacking force poured into Inchon and swiftly captured the city. The entire operation cost the United States only 21 dead, 174 wounded, and 1 missing.

At the same time, General Walker attacked the North Koreans in an attempt to break out of Pusan. With enemy forces in both the front and the rear, and in danger of losing their only supply line, the North Koreans were forced to relax their grip around Pusan. On September 22, Walker's troops broke through the enemy lines. By September 26, they were able to link up with the troops moving south from Inchon. Shortly thereafter, the American-led U.N. forces drove the North Koreans out of South Korea and pushed them back to the far corners of their own country.

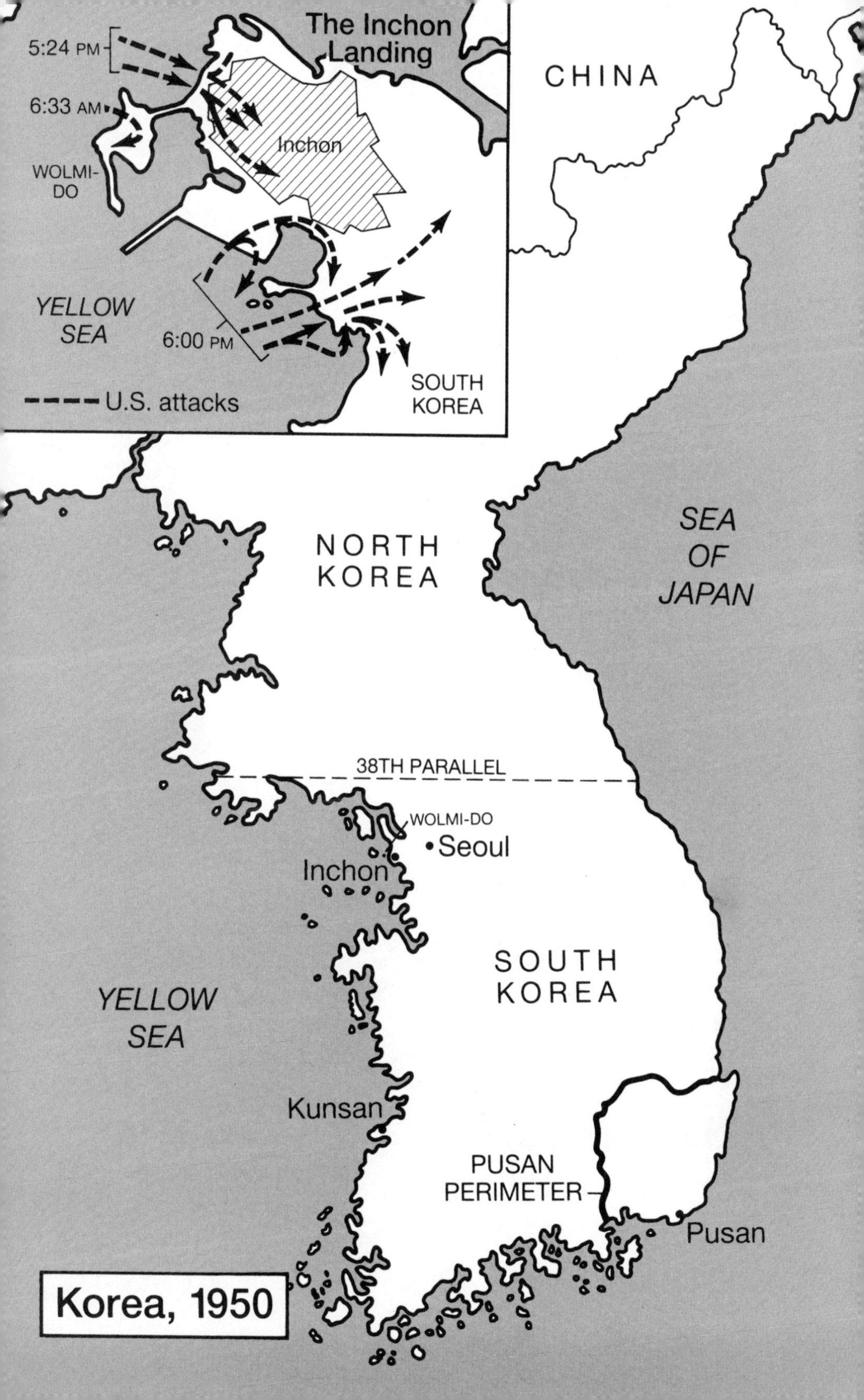
The Inchon Landing
5:24 PM
6:33 AM
WOLMI-DO
Inchon
YELLOW SEA
6:00 PM
SOUTH KOREA
U.S. attacks
CHINA
NORTH KOREA
SEA OF JAPAN
38TH PARALLEL
WOLMI-DO
Seoul
Inchon
YELLOW SEA
SOUTH KOREA
Kunsan
PUSAN PERIMETER
Pusan
Korea, 1950

ANALYSIS

MacArthur had luck on his side. Typhoon Kizia struck the Korean waters four days before the landing at Inchon. Had it arrived later, it might have disrupted the landing. In that case, MacArthur would have had a lot of explaining to do.

The judgment of historians is mixed as to whether the Inchon assault was crucial to the success of the United Nations' effort. There is some confusion as to the actual situation at the Pusan battle lines. Some believe that Walker's force was in such bad shape that it would not have been able to hold out against the North Koreans

Off the Korean coast, General MacArthur (seated, center) watches the Inchon landing unfold.

much longer. If so, the daring Inchon offensive saved Walker's army.

Others note that the North Korean offensive near Pusan had lost momentum and was not likely to go any further. The North Korean force turned out to be smaller than the U.N. observers had first estimated. There were probably no more than 70,000 North Koreans still on the attack. The defenders inside the Pusan perimeter may have outnumbered the attackers by 2 to 1 by the time MacArthur launched the Inchon offensive. Given that situation, he might have been able to make either of the other fighting options work.

Neither a concentration at Pusan nor a landing at Kunsan, however, would have achieved the quick, dramatic

Marines throw ladders up to scale the sea walls during the Inchon landing.

results of the Inchon landing. MacArthur's bold plan caught the North Koreans completely off guard, and his troops executed the plan brilliantly with a minimum of casualties. The successful attack on Inchon shattered any hopes the North Koreans had of capturing South Korea and guaranteed the safety of a battered army trapped near Pusan.

The Korean War entered a new phase when China rushed in to save the North Koreans from total defeat in late November 1950. The war ended up as more or less a stalemate. But that does not take away from the dramatic success of the Inchon landing, which many military analysts rate as MacArthur's finest campaign.

6

THE VIETNAMESE COMMUNIST FORCES

July 1967

Your armies have been fighting for nearly 25 years to establish an independent and united Vietnam under Communist leadership. Vietnam had been a colony of France for many years before Japan pushed the French out during World War II. As the Japanese war effort collapsed, your Communist party spearheaded a national independence movement that tried to take control of the nation.

Following the war, the French tried to reassert their dominance. Your group withdrew into the countryside and waged an ambush-and-hide campaign (known as guerrilla warfare) against them for several years. Gradually, you wore down the French with your persistence. In

1954, the French pulled out of Vietnam. However, the United States sided with non-Communists in the country and negotiated a treaty that divided the land into Communist North Vietnam and a Western-style democracy in South Vietnam, similar to what happened in Korea in the late 1940s. All sides agreed that the Vietnamese people be allowed to relocate to the section they preferred. Nearly 900,000 northerners moved south, while about 90,000 from South Vietnam moved north.

Your party, however, has never given up its effort to create a united Vietnam under Communist rule. Your escalating attacks on the South Vietnamese government in the early 1960s provoked an ever-greater response from its American allies, who were determined to stop the spread of Communism in Asia. In 1965, the United States began regularly bombing North Vietnamese cities and committed a large military force to the defense of South Vietnam.

In March 1965, U.S. marines hit the beach at Da Nang, South Vietnam.

For the past few years, you have returned to the guerrilla warfare methods that worked against the French, using the cover of the dense jungle. This has frustrated the American forces, who have continually called for reinforcements from back home to help them pin you down. But your guerrilla tactics have been costly to you. You have suffered far greater casualties than the enemy has. While you have not been driven out of South Vietnam, neither have you made much progress in achieving your objectives.

THE OPPOSING FORCES

More than a million anti-Communist soldiers patrol the narrow, 800-mile length of South Vietnam. This force includes more than 400,000 Americans, 340,000 trained troops of the regular South Vietnamese army, nearly 300,000 untrained local militia, and 60,000 soldiers from various countries such as Australia and South Korea. These soldiers have the advantage of the most modern aircraft, tanks, ships, bombs, artillery, transportation, and communications equipment in the world. The U.S. Navy dominates the sea that borders Vietnam on its eastern side. American aircraft control the skies well enough that your enemies can call in air support whenever they need it and can bomb your northern cities whenever they please.

The weak spot in the opposing forces could be the same one that ultimately defeated the French: commitment. The American government's stated goal of preventing the spread of Communism has not produced in its citizens the kind of impassioned dedication to the war that you hold. Many of the United States' own allies believe that the Americans should not be involved in this war. Although a majority of Americans support their government's defense of South Vietnam, there is a limit on the price they are willing to pay for defending a government halfway around the world.

As a result, Americans have tried to wage the war in a relatively cheap and painless manner. At first, they sent only advisers; then they provided support to the South Vietnamese troops. Finally, they ordered bombing campaigns. As you have stepped up your attacks, American involvement has increased. Determined to gain victory, the United States keeps shipping in more troops and equipment and engaging in more actual combat. More than 13,000 Americans have died in Vietnam since 1961, and the toll is accelerating. The price tag of the Vietnam War for Americans has risen to $20 billion per year.

The next year will be a crucial one for the American government in terms of holding the support of its people. During the presidential election year of 1968, the issue of support for the Vietnam policy will be a major issue in the campaign.

YOUR FORCES

Your soldiers are badly outnumbered in South Vietnam. About 240,000 fighters, the majority of them South Vietnamese Communists known as Vietcong, are stationed in South Vietnam. You can also draw on 450,000 regular army troops stationed in North Vietnam. You could also call up more recruits if necessary. Your

Chinese allies, who boast the largest standing army in the world, would probably come to your aid if the Americans invaded North Vietnam.

Although you receive substantial military supplies from China and the Soviet Union, you cannot begin to match the firepower of the enemy forces. Your armies have been able to survive in the face of such overwhelming strength by offering the enemy few visible targets. You have made use of the dense jungles to screen your movements and to evade pursuit. This has frustrated the Americans, who have often been unable to bring their superior weaponry into use.

You credit much of your success to your organization in the rural areas. You have developed excellent coordination between the main forces of your army, the small but active guerrilla units, and the local Communist sympathizers who live in South Vietnamese villages. This coordination allows you to attack secretly with a strong force, melt away when the enemy arrives, and then reappear when the enemy moves on.

Recently, however, you have lost some of your strength in the countryside. Ever since the escalation of the war in 1965, droves of rural South Vietnamese have been fleeing to the safety of cities. As nearly a million people per year have abandoned the rural lands, you are left with fewer local people to provide support, shelter, and manpower. This means that carrying on operations has become more difficult.

Nonetheless, your advisers calculate that you retain the manpower to continue the war indefinitely at the current level of fighting.

YOU ARE IN COMMAND.

What strategy will you use against the superior forces that stand in the way of your gaining control of South Vietnam?

Option 1 **Continue a low-level guerrilla war to wear down the Americans.**

You dare not escalate the war because putting many soldiers in full-scale battle against the Americans is dangerous. The more concentrated your forces, the bigger target they present for America's heavy firepower. One of your most experienced generals, Nguyen Chi Thanh, has warned, "If we fight the Americans in accordance with modern military tactics, we will be badly battered."

Instead, your objective should be to gradually wear down the Americans' will to continue the war, just as you wore down the French. Your advisers are unanimous in declaring that the Americans, like the French, do not like long and inconclusive wars. Your people, in contrast, have shown a relentless commitment. Already, they have fought for more than 20 years without losing sight of their goal, and they have repeatedly made whatever sacrifices have been asked of them for the sake of the effort. The fact that they have fewer riches than the Americans means your people have less to lose in a war. As one of your generals says, "We can endure the hardships of a lengthy war but they are unable to endure the hardships of war because they are a well-to-do people."

You already see signs that the Americans' patience is wearing thin, just as the French finally tired of this endless fighting. The American protest movement against the war is slowly growing. You can keep the pressure on by continuing to frustrate your enemies in the kind of war they hate. Guerrilla warfare ties down large numbers of enemy soldiers, limits the effectiveness of their firepower, and, according to your advisers, causes "tension and fear in him night and day, so that he sees the need to create a defense and a strong military force everywhere before he can become confident."

Time is on your side. Your strategy, then, should be to drag out the war as long as possible. You must avoid any large confrontation that will give the enemy a chance to claim a major victory.

Option 2 **Launch a massive surprise attack on dozens of South Vietnamese cities.**

On the surface, this may seem like a foolish strategy. It requires your troops to come out of the protection of the jungles into unfamiliar cities where their support has traditionally been the weakest. It exposes large pockets of your best guerrilla soldiers to the enormous firepower of the Americans. Also, it gives the Americans a chance to claim a dramatic victory that they can use to rally support for the war back home.

But, based on the "General Uprising" theory of your revolution, this option has several advantages. According to this theory, a sweeping offensive will catch your enemies by surprise and throw them into disarray. Your success will encourage the masses of people in South Vietnamese cities who have been too intimidated by the power of the United States to join your cause. They will rise up and fight alongside your soldiers in a general uprising that will overthrow the government of South Vietnam.

Of course, you have no guarantee that the masses of people in the cities will join you. Actually, many of them fear communism. Others, however, would like their land to be free of all foreigners. Still others do not trust the current South Vietnamese administration and might be led to support a united, liberated Vietnam.

Even if the general uprising is only partially successful, it could still serve a useful purpose. American leaders have been trying to maintain support at home for the war by claiming they are close to decisive victory. In reality, your forces still control large sections of the countryside. A massive, coordinated assault on targets all over South Vietnam will prove to the Americans that you are far from beaten. Such an assault will warn them that they face a long, bloody fight if they stay in Vietnam. This further escalation of the war will force the Americans either to increase their war effort or to think about pulling out of Vietnam. In an election year, war-weary Americans may well put the pressure on their president to get out.

Option 3 **Concentrate your forces in a single surprise attack against a single target.**

The small-scale guerrilla warfare of ***Option 1*** may not be enough to defeat the enemy because this tactic may not cost the Americans and their allies enough to discourage them from staying in the war. Moreover, an all-out attack may not produce a general uprising. Thus ***Option 2*** presents an enormous risk. If the massive attack on dozens of South Vietnamese cities fails, you could end up destroying a large portion of your organization in South Vietnam.

Option 3 could deal the desired shocking blow to the spirits of the American people without all of the risk involved in ***Option 2***. What's more, this third option employs the basic strategy that proved effective in your previous war against the French.

Back in the 1950s, your forces used a combination of guerrilla activity and conventional forces to keep the pressure on the French. Your ambush-and-hide attacks stretched the French forces thin while the occasional battles exacted the casualties that discouraged France's reluctant supporters. You achieved final victory in that war by fighting a major battle at Dien Bien Phu. Although you suffered heavy casualties in that battle, you succeeded in capturing 10,000 French soldiers. This defeat so discouraged the French that they decided once and for all that the war was not worth the cost.

Option 3, however, may have less chance of success than ***Option 2***. A massive, nationwide attack on South Vietnamese cities would at least stretch and scatter the defensive forces of South Vietnam as they attempt to put out these uprisings. That means the Americans would not be able to mass their power against any one spot. In contrast, a concentrated attack on a single location would present an inviting target that would attract the full force of American firepower. You cannot rely on history to make this decision for you. The American forces are far stronger than the French ever were in the 1950s.

Communist soldiers march their French prisoners from Dien Bien Phu in May 1954, marking the end of France's involvement in Vietnam.

Option 4 **Recognize that you are outmatched and recommend a negotiated peace.**

Perhaps you have bitten off more than you can chew this time. Your military forces are not nearly as strong as the German or Japanese armies that the United States helped defeat in World War II. What makes you think you have any chance of succeeding where those two powers failed? Americans are fond of boasting that they have never lost a war. Their pride will not let them give up.

Perhaps it would be better to take advantage of American uneasiness about the war by pushing for the best peace you can get. Americans are groping for an escape from this mess, so this may be the best time to deal. Americans may be so eager for a way out that they will give you favorable terms—perhaps even more territory. The American president, Lyndon Johnson, may be especially eager to deal so he can boost his chances of reelection.

THE DECISION IS YOURS
WHAT WILL YOU DO?

Option 1 **Continue a low-level guerrilla war to wear down the Americans.**

Option 2 **Launch a massive surprise attack on dozens of South Vietnamese cities.**

Option 3 **Concentrate your forces in a single surprise attack against a single target.**

Option 4 **Recognize that you are outmatched and recommend a negotiated peace.**

The Communist Vietnamese military leaders chose *Option 2.*

The major military decisions of the Vietnamese Communists were decided in secret by a tight circle of leaders. They have left the world scant documentation of their reasons for taking the actions they did.

What is known, however, is that in July 1967 they approved the largest offensive action of the war. Their plan called for a simultaneous surprise attack on nearly every significant city and town in South Vietnam. To ensure that these attacks came as a total surprise, the Communists scheduled them to occur during the celebration of the Lunar New Year, known as Tet, at the end of January. Ever since 1963, the Communists had declared a ceasefire in honor of this important week-long celebration. In late January 1968, they would proclaim another Tet ceasefire and then attack during that time.

During their six months of preparation, the Communists laid plans for their attack and smuggled weapons, ammunition, and other supplies to points near the targets they had selected. They assigned about 67,000 of their 240,000 troops in South Vietnam to the action. They were almost exclusively Vietcong rather than North Vietnamese regulars.

Vietnam's Communist leader, Ho Chi Minh (1890-1969), organized guerrilla forces to fight the Japanese in the 1940s, the French in the 1950s, and the Americans in the 1960s, to free his country from foreign domination.

RESULT

On January 30, 1968, the Communists attacked 7 towns. Possibly these were premature attacks due to missed communication. The next day, however, they stormed more than 100 cities and towns throughout South Vietnam, including Saigon, the capital of the country.

The Tet Offensive caught the Americans and South Vietnamese completely by surprise, despite the fact that American intelligence had uncovered evidence that the Communists were planning a large offensive. Americans were convinced that the offensive would take the form of a large strike along the border regions ***(Option 3)*** and were preparing to deal with that. A massive attack against the cities struck the Americans as such an outrageous gamble that in the words of one, "If we'd gotten the whole battle plan, it wouldn't have been believed."

With this initial advantage, the Communists smashed into the cities and achieved some successes. They captured the city of Hue, and a small group of commandos broke into the U.S. Embassy in Saigon.

But the general uprising never came about. In every case, the Communists were thrown back, often with heavy losses. With the exception of a bitter, 25-day struggle to recapture Hue, American and South Vietnamese forces quickly gained control of every city that the Communists had targeted. During the Tet Offensive, more than 58,000 Communist soldiers were killed, along with 5,000 South Vietnamese regulars, 4,000 Americans, and over 12,000 civilians.

ANALYSIS

The Tet Offensive was, in the words of one Vietcong participant, a "military debacle" that dashed the Communists' hopes for a sudden victory. According to this source, "The truth was that Tet cost us half of our forces. Our losses were so immense that we were simply unable to replace them." Many of those killed were experienced, dedicated jungle fighters who would be sadly missed in the years to come. These losses, which would cost the Communists dearly, forced them to rely more on regular North Vietnamese troops instead of guerrillas.

At the height of the Tet Offensive, U.S. marines take cover from and return sniper fire in the street-by-street battle to recapture Hue.

The Tet Offensive also dealt a blow to the prestige of the Communists in the south. Their claim to be the popular liberators of Vietnam rang hollow in the face of their failure to produce a general uprising. Worse yet, the Tet attacks scared the South Vietnamese into doubling the size of their army. The combination of these factors meant that by 1969 the South Vietnamese government enjoyed its strongest position in years.

But there was another side to the story. As North Vietnamese General Vo Nguyen Giap later said, "For us there is no such thing as a single strategy. The Tet Offensive had multiple objectives." While it failed to accomplish its main military objective, it gained something even more important. The Johnson administration had led Americans to believe the situation in Vietnam was finally just about under control and that the war would soon be won. Suddenly, in every corner of South Vietnam, this "defeated enemy" burst out in well-coordinated attacks that killed 4,000 Americans. If the situation was under control, the shocked American public asked, why could its troops and leaders not even keep the enemy out of America's embassy building in Saigon?

The sense of futility and despair that followed Tet shattered the credibility of the Johnson administration. In November 1967, 50 percent of Americans believed the United States was winning the war, and only 8 percent thought they were losing. Following Tet, only 33 percent thought the United States was winning, while 23 percent thought America was losing. The Tet Offensive had turned the tide of public opinion against continued involvement in this confusing foreign war.

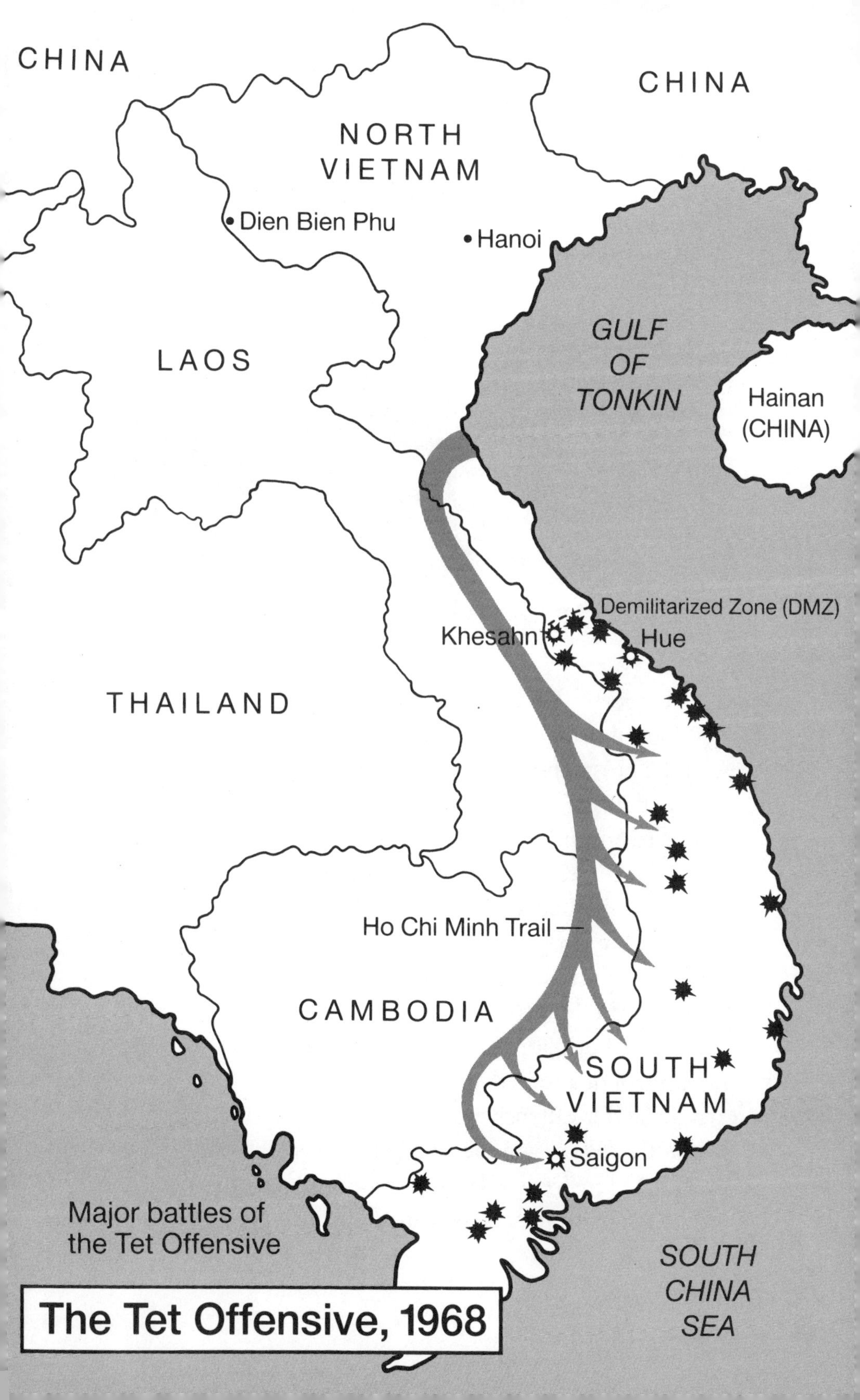
CHINA
CHINA
NORTH VIETNAM
Dien Bien Phu
Hanoi
GULF OF TONKIN
Hainan (CHINA)
LAOS
Demilitarized Zone (DMZ)
Khesahn
Hue
THAILAND
Ho Chi Minh Trail
CAMBODIA
SOUTH VIETNAM
Saigon
Major battles of the Tet Offensive
SOUTH CHINA SEA
The Tet Offensive, 1968

Vo Nguyen Giap, longtime military aide to Ho Chi Minh, served North Vietnam as both minister of defense and commander-in-chief. Years before he planned the Tet Offensive, he directed the Communist victory at Dien Bien Phu.

Under criticism from members of his own party, Lyndon Johnson did not seek reelection. Richard Nixon won the presidency and began a gradual process of shifting the fighting responsibility in Vietnam from American troops to South Vietnamese troops. In 1973, the United States concluded a peace treaty with the Communists and pulled out of Vietnam.

Within two years, North Vietnamese forces, backed by increasing military aid from the Soviet Union, overwhelmed the South Vietnamese armies. They captured Saigon on April 30, 1975, completing their 30-year fight for control of a united Vietnam.

The Tet Offensive turned out to be a case of losing the battle only to win the war. The decision to authorize the Tet Offensive was largely responsible for paving the way to a Communist victory in Vietnam.

7

The Coalition Forces of Operation Desert Storm

February 1991

Last summer, Iraq launched a sudden and brutal invasion of its tiny neighbor, Kuwait. The Iraqi forces easily captured this oil-rich country and threw the Middle East into turmoil.

Iraq's dictator, Saddam Hussein, had used oil revenues to build an enormous, well-equipped army. He has shown himself all too eager to use this force to solidify his control in Iraq and to gain any advantage possible against his enemies. Prior to the plundering of Kuwait, he had waged a costly war with Iran. His troops had resorted to chemical warfare in this fight. Your intelligence sources collected evidence that Iraq is close to developing more terrible weapons— nuclear bombs. The threat that Iraq poses to other nations in the region, particularly Saudi Arabia, alarmed many countries of the world. Led by the United States, 28 nations formed a military coalition to enforce a United Nations resolution calling for the withdrawal of Iraqi troops from Kuwait. Saddam Hussein, however, refused to yield.

For six months the coalition armies mustered their forces near the southern border of Kuwait while the Iraqis dug in and constructed elaborate defenses. On the night of January 16, the skies lit up with missiles and bombs as the coalition aircraft and naval forces mounted their first attack. The coalition quickly destroyed Iraqi communications systems and gained total domination of the air. For the past few weeks, your planes have been bombing

Quickly into Operation Desert Storm, coalition aircraft such as this U.S. A-10A Thunderbolt II *dominated the skies over Iraq and Kuwait.*

targets virtually without resistance. Hundreds of missions per day have dropped tons of explosives on the Iraqi defensive positions. The Iraqis, unable to defend themselves against these attacks, have suffered severely. Yet Saddam Hussein shows no signs of withdrawing from Kuwait.

As the air war stretches on into mid-February, there is no question which side has the greater military might. The only question is how much will a victory cost the coalition? Saddam Hussein believes that if he can make the price high enough, the coalition will abandon the fight. Therefore, he is determined to inflict as much death as possible on the coalition. He has shown a willingness in the past to sacrifice hundreds of thousands of his soldiers in exchange for the blood of his enemies.

THE OPPOSING FORCES

Although Iraq is only a moderate-sized Third World nation, it boasts the fourth largest military force in the world. More than half a million Iraqi soldiers are stationed in and around Kuwait. At the start of the war, they were equipped with more than 4,200 tanks, 3,100 pieces of artillery, and 2,800 armored vehicles. The bombing missions have certainly reduced that number, but no one knows precisely how much damage the Iraqis have sustained.

The Iraqis have constructed a three-layered defense of Kuwait. The first line consists of a no man's land of barbed wire, tank traps, and hundreds of thousands of mines, backed up by infantry divisions. These frontline troops are the most inexperienced, poorly trained, and poorly equipped in the Iraqi army.

A second line of soldiers is spread across the interior of Kuwait to counterattack any coalition forces that survive the mine fields and break through the front lines. Should any forces break through the second line, they will run into the heart of the Iraqi defense. The Republican Guards, Iraq's best soldiers, are dug in just north of the Kuwaiti border. These 150,000 soldiers are armed with modern Soviet tanks and artillery.

Many of the Iraqi soldiers in the second and third lines of defense are hardened combat veterans who gained experience while fighting the Iranians. In recent years, American military experts have rated Iraq's armored divisions as among the best in the world—better than the forces of Israel, Great Britain, and even the Soviet Union. The Iraqis have fought especially well when defending themselves against attack. This is a defensive battle for them, and they have had six months to prepare for it.

You had expected Iraq's air defenses to be moderately strong, but they turned out to be vastly overrated. In the early days of the air war, the Iraqi pilots were so thoroughly outclassed that they do not even risk taking to the air anymore. This lack of air support puts Iraq at a huge disadvantage.

The coalition forces have little respect for Saddam Hussein as a military mastermind. But they worry that he may have some unconventional tricks to play. Of gravest concern are the chemical and biological weapons that Iraq has stockpiled. Saddam Hussein has used them in the past and will likely use them against the attacking forces.

YOUR FORCES

The combined military might of the coalition nations far surpasses that of Iraq. However, you are saddled with the problem of transporting these forces thousands of miles and then organizing them in a faraway land. The enormous challenge of trying to coordinate the activities of 18 different armies that do not speak the same language further compounds the difficulty.

Despite your frantic efforts in the past six months, you have not been able to assemble an overwhelming ground force. In order to have any chance for success, an invading force normally should be larger than a well-entrenched defensive army. The coalition armies, however, have only 450,000 soldiers in the field, about 100,000 fewer than the Iraqis. When you count only actual combat troops, as opposed to support troops, the Iraqi advantage may be even larger. Furthermore, few of the coalition soldiers have been tested in battle. The coalition forces probably hold the edge in tanks, depending on how many Iraqi tanks have been destroyed by bombing.

The coalition relies heavily on its overwhelming advantage in technology. The air war demonstrated how decisive high-tech weaponry can be. "Stealth" planes proved they could evade radar detection. American aircraft further tied up Iraqi radar with sophisticated electronic jamming until air strikes knocked out these radar installations. Cruise missiles launched from ships in the Persian Gulf performed effectively. "Smart" bombs, which home in on a laser beam reflected off the target, proved so precise that, in several cases, they entered the actual air shafts of a bomb shelter.

Your ground forces have similar high-tech weaponry, although much of it has not been battle tested. Your total command of the air gives your ground forces a huge advantage. The constant bombing keeps the Iraqis from observing your army's position and movements. They are forced to bury their tanks and artillery in the sand to prevent them from being destroyed by air raids, which limits the use of their equipment against a ground attack.

Your navy also patrols the Persian Gulf alongside Kuwait, unopposed. These ships provide launching bases for aircraft and can fill the sky with deadly missiles and artillery fire.

U.S. soldiers aboard an M-3 Bradley *fighting vehicle patrol the Saudi desert.*

One of the most sophisticated weapons in the U.S. arsenal, an F-117 *"Stealth" fighter lands after completing a mission during Operation Desert Storm.*

YOU ARE IN COMMAND.

Saddam Hussein is determined not to leave Kuwait without making you pay a bloody price in what he claims will be "the mother of all battles." How will you force his troops out of Kuwait without paying too steep a price?

Option 1 **Rely totally on your air power.**

Air Force General Michael Dugan believes that air power is the only answer you need. You've got a good thing going. Why change it? The ease with which coalition pilots have been blasting targets from a safe distance has caused some to label this the "Nintendo War." Why expose your ground troops to Iraq's murderous defenses

U.S. pilots under the command of General Michael Dugan, air force chief of staff, pounded Iraqi positions day after day, virtually without opposition.

when you can pulverize the Iraqi positions day after day with little risk to any of your own soldiers?

Some analysts estimate that your air offensive has already destroyed between one-fourth and one-half of the Iraqi tanks and artillery. If you keep the pressure on, sooner or later you will so decimate the Iraqi army that it will either have to surrender or be so crippled that your ground forces will be able to stroll through Kuwait.

The air war presents virtually no risk to your soldiers. The Iraqis are rarely able to shoot down a single plane in a day. Their army's only hope of survival is to dig in deeply enough to escape the bombing damage. If the troops try to come out of their holes to attack you, your air force would wipe them out.

One problem with this approach is that you cannot measure with any certainty the effectiveness of the bombing. The Iraqi troops are firmly entrenched in their sand bunkers. Many of them may be so protected that no amount of bombing will destroy them.

Also, bombing is a slow method of achieving final victory in a war. Even a successful air campaign might last several months. This would drag the war on into the hot season that will return to the desert in another month or so. Your ground forces will then be sitting in an oven along the Kuwaiti border. March also brings the return of high winds that kick up dust storms. In a desert with no landmarks and no windbreaks, these storms blot out all visibility. Troops could easily get lost and confused, especially if the Iraqis launch an attack.

Option 2 **Hit Iraqi-occupied Kuwait head-on with a massive ground assault.**

General Colin Powell believes the air force cannot do the job alone. The dug-in Iraqis will simply take cover for as long as you want to bomb them. According to one military expert, "The only way an army buys real estate and wins wars is with infantry on the ground."

Normally, a head-on assault against an entrenched enemy with a larger army would be suicide. Coalition forces must advance slowly and carefully through the mine fields. Such an advance makes them easy targets for Iraqi soldiers.

But many believe the Iraqis are staggering from the air force pounding they have endured. In small skirmishes near the front lines, dozens of shell-shocked Iraqi soldiers have surrendered eagerly at the first opportunity. Military expert David Hackworth believes that the Iraqis are ready "to cut and run." The Iraqis are hanging on by a thread as it is. A massive show of force will break it.

Even if the Iraqis have some fight left in them, the coalition's advantage in air power and in modern equipment will overwhelm them. Look what the high-tech gadgetry of the air force did to the supposedly capable Iraqi air defenses and air forces. The ground forces' weaponry will show the same superiority. This is not like Vietnam, where the enemy could escape American firepower by melting into the jungle. The desert provides your enemies with nothing to cover their movements.

A quick, massive attack also has the advantage of concentrating your forces in a small area, which minimizes the problem of supplying a huge army in the desert. On the negative side, the frontal assault is potentially the most deadly for your army. Experts predict that even a successful attack could cost the lives of 200 of your soldiers every hour. This plays into Saddam Hussein's hands by giving him the bloody battle he is looking for. You must never underestimate the damage that a well-prepared enemy can inflict. Your 3,500 tanks may seem like an unstoppable force. But you need to remember that Israel lost 1,500 tanks in two weeks during its 1973 war with Arab countries.

Furthermore, the Iraqis may have suffered less than you think from the air war. They have set up thousands of dummy tanks and other decoy targets in the sand. Your estimates of the numbers of targets your air force has destroyed could be way off. The Iraqis could be waiting for you with most of their firepower still intact.

***Option 3* Stage an amphibious landing from the Persian Gulf.**

The tactic of a frontal assault ***(Option 2)*** has been outdated for more than 100 years. Modern weapons simply lay down too thick a wall of ammunition for any mass of troops to get through. The Iraqi soldiers have turned Kuwait into a giant killing field, and they are praying for you to come at them.

You could avoid that three-layered defense and those minefields by ordering the type of assault that made General MacArthur famous: the amphibious assault. The Persian Gulf washes right up to the shores of Kuwait City. A large contingent of marines is waiting to seize the beaches behind the enemy front lines and liberate the city.

You could use the usual method of amphibious assault: Begin with a thorough bombardment and follow that by rushing the beaches. The ground forces along the south and west of Kuwait could engage in "holding attacks"—cautious advances that go close enough to enemy troops to engage them in battle without actually trying to break through the lines. This would tie up the Iraqi forces so they could not reinforce their defenders on the beaches.

The marines making this attack would enjoy some advantages that were not available to those who captured Inchon in the Korean War. You can now transport the

A Tomahawk missile leaves the USS Missouri *en route to an Iraqi target.*

marines in hovercraft that can skim rapidly over both water and land. The most powerful air force ever assembled would cover the attack.

The amphibious assault, however, is always a risk because this tactic exposes the attacking troops on the surface of the water for a dangerous period of time. The Inchon attack had the advantage of surprise. The Iraqis, though, are fully aware that you could attack from that side, and they have prepared for it. They have caused an enormous offshore oil spill that has spread 7 million gallons of oil across the path of the marines. There also are rumors that the Iraqis have installed high-voltage power lines in the water near the beach area to electrocute any soldiers attempting to land.

Option 4 **Try an end-run around the Iraqi defenses and crush them from behind.**

You can't expect your air force to win the war by itself, and both a frontal assault and an amphibious assault could face fierce resistance. With a bit of daring, though, you could race through the desert in a wide arc around the northwest side of the battle lines. By choosing that battleground, you avoid the minefields and other prepared Iraqi defenses. If you move fast enough, you could surprise the Iraqis and surround their entire army.

This option takes advantage of one of the strengths of your ground forces—the speed of your *M-1A1 Abrams* tanks. These vehicles can speed across the desert landscape at over 45 miles per hour.

Coalition ground forces relied heavily on their armor, including the M-1A1 Abrams *tank, here laying a smoke screen.*

However, in order to make this option effective, you will need to pull a large portion of your forces out of the main battlefront and shift them far to the west. This will leave your front lines dangerously thin. Should the Iraqis attack, they might be able to break through and cut off the main part of your army from its supplies. Supply lines are crucial in a desert war. Germany's General Erwin Rommel made rapid advances in North Africa during World War II, only to be defeated when his supplies ran out.

The danger of an Iraqi attack, though, is slight. The hunkered-down Iraqis are not in a good position to attack. They do not want to expose themselves to coalition bombers. Also, with their air force completely grounded, the Iraqis have no way of knowing what you are planning. Under normal conditions, the movement of 200,000 troops from one part of the battle front to another would be difficult to conceal. But the Iraqis are fighting blind.

A more serious concern is the danger of an end run outrunning your own supplies. A single tank division guzzles half a million gallons of fuel and 300,000 gallons of water per day. By stretching the battle lines far to the west, you stretch your supply lines ever further. That western stretch of desert has no roads for supply trucks to travel. The hard desert floor is strewn with sharp, flat stones that wreak havoc on tires. In order to ensure supplies, you would have to airdrop supply depots behind enemy lines and hope the enemy did not find and destroy them.

Another problem is that the desert sand is brutal on mechanical equipment. The fine grit gets everywhere and can clog moving parts and foul electrical systems in no time. Your motorized vehicles have been changing filters every day in an effort to keep them working. Large-scale failure of equipment would leave much of your firepower stranded and useless in the desert.

THE DECISION IS YOURS
WHAT WILL YOU DO?

Option 1 **Rely totally on your air power.**

Option 2 **Hit Iraqi-occupied Kuwait head-on with a massive ground assault.**

Option 3 **Stage an amphibious landing from the Persian Gulf.**

Option 4 **Try an end-run around the Iraqi defenses and crush them from behind.**

West Point graduate and Vietnam veteran General H. Norman Schwarzkopf commanded the multinational coalition forces that opposed Iraqi dictator Saddam Hussein.

General H. Norman Schwarzkopf, commander of the coalition forces, chose *Option 4*.

Schwarzkopf remembered from the Vietnam War that Vietcong soldiers would "just pop up from their heavy bombing bunkers once the planes had gone." That led him to dismiss the idea that air power alone could win the war as "a bunch of hoo-hah."

He believed that a prime rule of war was "never underestimate an enemy's strength." He had to assume the Iraqi army was as good as advertised. That made him wary of the frontal assault—a dangerous and potentially bloody course of action.

Schwarzkopf chose the end-run over the amphibious assault, a choice that he confessed was a gamble. He referred to the plan as a "Hail Mary" play, named after the football strategy in which a desperate team throws the ball up for grabs and hopes one of its players comes down with the ball. The risks that Schwarzkopf took—weakening his center lines, extending his supply lines, and getting a main force caught in the desert—were especially dangerous when facing a larger army.

His decision was shaped in part by his contempt for Saddam Hussein's military expertise. The Iraqi leader had shown little understanding of basic war strategy or tactics, which led Schwarzkopf to believe he could get away with a bold flanking maneuver.

In the days before the attack, Schwarzkopf repositioned nearly a quarter of a million troops to the west. At the same time, he pretended to try an amphibious assault on Kuwait's east coast to draw Iraq's attention away from his plan.

On February 24, Schwarzkopf sent his tanks across the thinly guarded western border of Iraq. The coalition landed paratroopers and fuel supplies far behind enemy lines in Iraq. Coalition forces also advanced against the first line of Iraqi defenses along the southern border of Kuwait.

RESULT

With their supply system keeping fuel, water, and ammunition flowing, the tanks sped quickly to the rear of Iraq's Republican Guards. They drew the surprised Iraqis into a major tank battle and completely routed them. This tactic sealed off the entire Iraqi army from escape. Flushed out into the open, the Iraqis were defenseless against the coalition aircraft that swarmed in the sky.

Meanwhile, coalition forces attacking Iraq's front lines met little resistance. Iraqi soldiers surrendered in massive numbers. The "mother of all battles" proved to be a 100-hour slaughter, one of the most one-sided battles in history. At a cost of a few armored vehicles and 150 casualties, the coalition forces drove Iraq out of Kuwait, destroying more than 2,000 Iraqi tanks and reducing the Iraqi army to shambles.

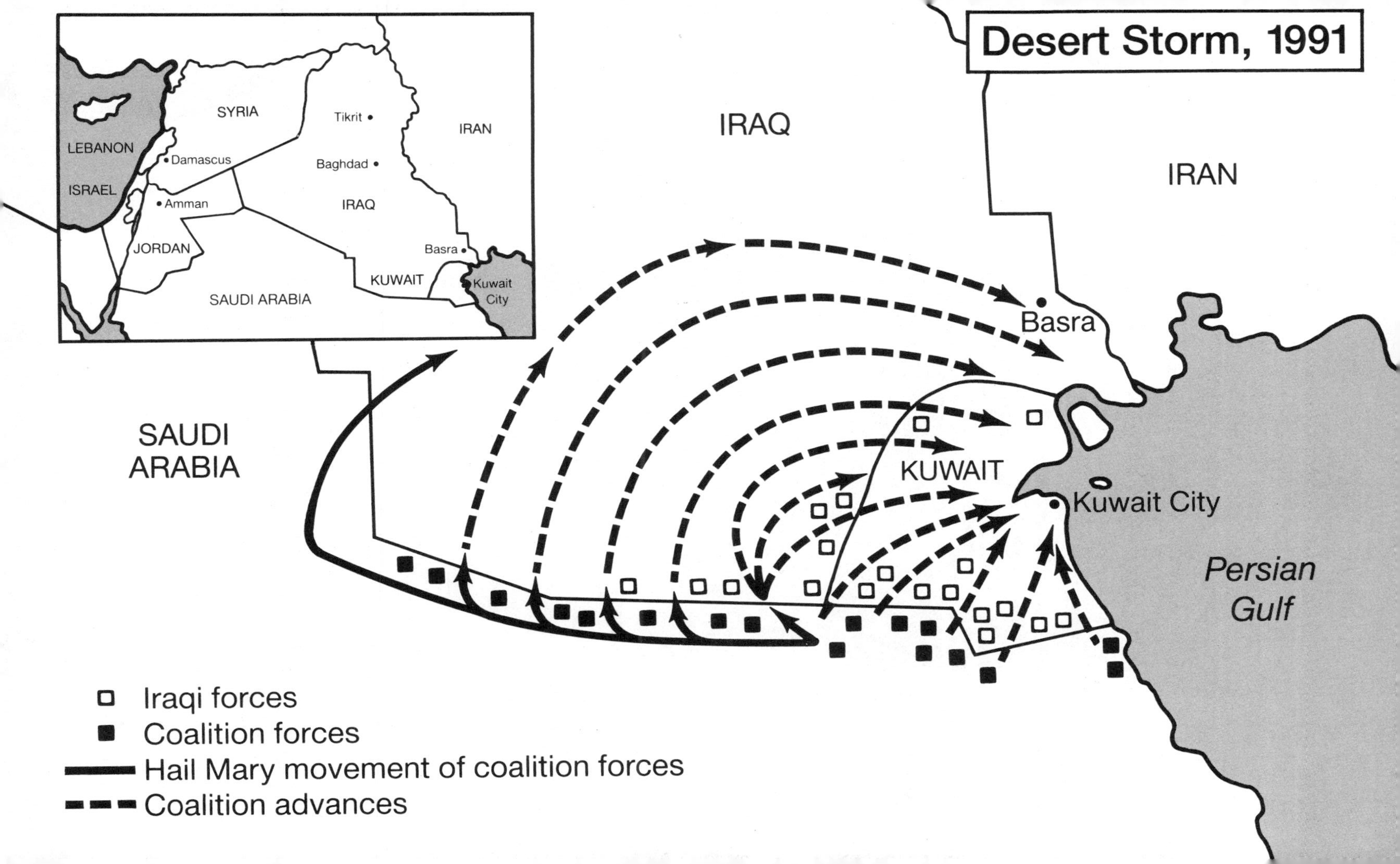

Desert Storm, 1991
IRAQ
IRAN
SAUDI ARABIA
Basra
KUWAIT
Kuwait City
Persian Gulf
SYRIA
LEBANON
ISRAEL
JORDAN
Damascus
Amman
Tikrit
Baghdad
Kuwait City
Iraqi forces
Coalition forces
Hail Mary movement of coalition forces
Coalition advances

An Iraqi tank column stands devastated in the Euphrates River valley near the city of Basra.

ANALYSIS

"The reality is that they [the Iraqi army] were nowhere near as tough as we gave them credit for," Schwarzkopf later said. One military analyst downplayed the effect of Schwarzkopf's strategy, saying that air power had virtually won the war by itself. Events proved that the coalition forces, with their technological advantage and control of

Kuwait is free, and the joyous victors wave flags to celebrate.

the skies, were so superior they could have defeated Iraq any number of ways.

Nonetheless, the end-run was a master stroke. The maneuver caught Iraq by surprise and destroyed whatever chance it had to inflict heavy casualties. The Republican Guards, the most dangerous element of the Iraqi force,

The architects of Iraqi defeat, General Schwarzkopf and the chairman of the Joint Chiefs of Staff, General Colin Powell (left), enjoy a Middle Eastern beverage.

were caught facing the wrong way, allowing the coalition forces to destroy many Iraqi tanks from the rear.

The extremely light coalition casualties, which Schwarzkopf called "almost miraculous," were in a large part due to a daring, well-conceived, and masterfully executed strategy.

Source Notes

Quoted passages are noted by page and order of citation:

pp. 8, 68: Mitsuo Fuchido, *Midway, The Battle That Doomed Japan: The Japanese Navy's Story* (Annapolis: U.S. Naval Institute, 1955.)

pp. 14, 28: Lt. Col. Joseph B. Mitchell and Sir Edward Creasy, *Twenty Decisive Battles of the World* (New York: Macmillan, 1964.)

p. 26: Henri Isselin, *The Battle of the Marne* (Garden City, NY: Doubleday, 1966.)

pp. 37, 43: Laurence Thompson, *1940* (New York: Morrow, 1981.)

p. 40 (1st): Stephen Sears, *World War II: The Best of American Heritage* (Boston: Houghton Mifflin, 1991.)

p. 40 (2nd): H.A. Jacobsen and J. Rohwer, eds., *Decisive Battles of World War II: The German View* (New York: Putnam, 1965.)

pp. 79, 85 (1st), 90 (2nd): David Eisenhower, *Eisenhower at War, 1943-45* (New York: Random House, 1986.)

pp. 85 (2nd, 3rd), 88, 90 (1st): Martin Blumenson, *Eisenhower* (New York: Ballantine, 1972.)

pp. 96, 103 (1st, 3rd): D. Clayton James, *The Years of MacArthur* (Boston: Houghton Mifflin, 1976.)

pp. 100, 103 (2nd): Michael Langley, *Inchon Landing: MacArthur's Last Triumph* (New York: Times Books, 1979.)

pp. 114, 115, 123, 124: Don Oberlin, *Tet* (New York: Doubleday, 1971.)

pp. 135, 136, 143 (2nd): David Hackworth, "We'll Win But. . . ," *Newsweek* (January 21, 1991.)

p. 143 (1st): "A Second Look at the Airwar," *Newsweek* (January 7, 1991.)

pp. 143 (3rd), 146, 148: C.D.B. Bryan "Desert Norm," *Reader's Digest* (June 1991.)

p. 143 (4th): "The 100 Hour War," *U.S. News & World Report* (March 14, 1991.)

BIBLIOGRAPHY

Blumenson, Martin. *Eisenhower.* New York: Ballantine, 1972.

Bryan, C.D.B. "Desert Norm," *Reader's Digest,* June 1991.

Eisenhower, David. *Eisenhower at War, 1943-45.* New York: Random House, 1986.

Fuchida, Mitsuo. *Midway, The Battle that Doomed Japan: The Japanese Navy's Story.* Annapolis: United States Naval Institute, 1955.

Hackworth, David. "We'll Win But. . . ," *Newsweek,* January 21, 1991.

Isselin, Henri. *The Battle of The Marne.* Garden City, NY: Doubleday, 1966.

Jacobsen, H.A. and J. Rohwer, eds. *Decisive Battles of World War II: The German View.* New York: Putman, 1965.

James, D. Clayton. *The Years of MacArthur.* Boston: Houghton Mifflin, 1976.

Karnow, Stanley. *Vietnam: A History.* New York: Viking, 1983.

Langley, Michael. *Inchon Landing: MacArthur's Last Triumph.* New York: Times Books, 1979.

Lewin, Ronald. *Hitler's Mistakes.* New York: William Morrow, 1984.

Mitchell, Joseph and Sir Edward Creasy. *Twenty Decisive Battles of the World.* New York: Macmillan, 1964.

Newsweek, January 7, 1991.

Oberlin, Don. *Tet.* New York: Doubleday, 1971.

Sears, Stephen. *World War II: The Best of American Heritage.* Boston: Houghton Mifflin, 1991.

Stokesbury, James L. *A Short History of the Korean War.* New York: William Morrow, 1988.

Taylor, Theodore. *The Battle of Midway Island.* New York: Avon, 1981.

Thompson, Laurence. *1940.* New York: Morrow, 1981.

U.S. News & World Report, March 14, 1991.

INDEX

Photo Credits

Photographs courtesy of the Library of Congress: pp. 6, 42, 84; Bundesarchiv, Germany, pp. 10, 16; National Archives, pp. 20, 22, 31, 34, 44, 46, 57, 59, 61, 63, 68, 72, 74, 81, 83, 87; Dwight D. Eisenhower Library, pp. 77, 90; MacArthur Memorial, pp. 95, 101, 102, 106, 107; The Bettmann Archive, pp. 110, 118, 121, 123, 126; U.S. Department of Defense, pp. 128, 132, 133, 134, 138, 139, 142, 146, 147, 148.

ABOUT THE AUTHOR

NATHAN AASENG is a widely published author of books for young readers. He has covered a diverse range of subjects, including history, biography, social issues, sports, health, business, science, and fiction. Twenty of his books have won awards from organizations such as the national Council for Social Studies, National Science Teachers Association, International Reading Association, Junior Library Guild, and the Child Study Association of America. Aaseng is the author of *Great Justices of the Supreme Court*, *You Are the President*, and the forthcoming books, *You Are the Justice*, and *You Are the President II: 1800-1899*. He lives in Eau Claire, Wisconsin, with his wife and children.